the
Foodscape
Revolution

the Foodscape Revolution

*Finding a Better Way to Make Space
for Food and Beauty in Your Garden*

Brie Arthur

st. lynn's
press

Pittsburgh

The Foodscape Revolution

Finding a Better Way to Make Space for Food and Beauty in Your Garden

ISBN-13: 978-1-943366-18-7

Library of Congress Control Number: 2016958269
CIP information available upon request

First Edition, 2017

St. Lynn's Press . POB 18680 . Pittsburgh, PA 15236
412.381.9933 . www.stlynnspress.com

Book design – Holly Rosborough • Senior Editor – Catherine Dees
Editor – Morgan Stout • Horticultural Editor – Katie Elzer-Peters
Illustrations – Preston Montague

Photo credits:
All photos © Brie Arthur, except for the following:
Katie Elzer-Peters: pages 24 (left), 44 (right), 62 (right), 64 (left), 70 (left), 73 (left), 74, 76 (left), 77 (left), 83 (right), 84 (left), 85 (left), 89, 118, 135, 136, 137, 150, 152, 153, 155 (right); DL Anderson, page 187; David Arthur, page 146, Tower Garden, page 143; Mark Hyland, page 111; Joe Lamp'l, page 189; Troy B. Marden, pages 114 and 119; Carol Reese, page 139; Jeremy Schmidt, page 168; Prudy Smith, pages 29 and 151; Burpee®, page 66; page 63, Bok Choy, © js (Wikimedia, https://upload.wikimedia.org/wikipedia/commons/5/58/Bok_Choy.JPG)

Printed in Canada
on certified FSC recycled paper using soy-based inks

This title and all of St. Lynn's Press books may be purchased for educational, business or sales promotional use. For information please write:
Special Markets Department . St. Lynn's Press . POB 18680 . Pittsburgh, PA 15236

10 9 8 7 6 5 4 3 2

To my loving husband, David Arthur,
and neighborhood garden helpers Aidan and Abby DelGatto.

Your inspiration can be seen in every landscape
that embraces beauty and bounty.

Thank you for your unwavering support,
hard work and laughter.

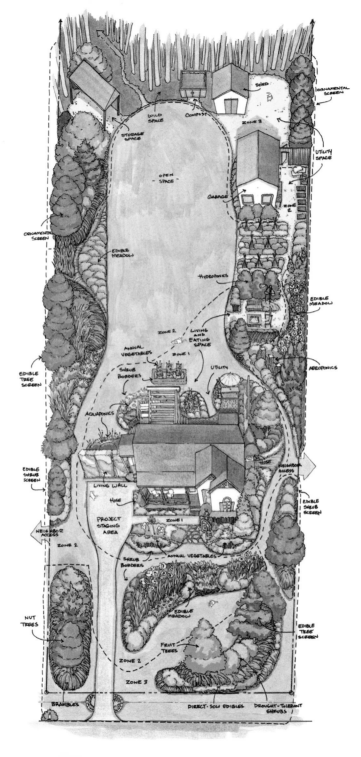

Here is my own Foodscape. I used a scaled drawing converted from my property plot plan as my base map.

Table of Contents

INTRODUCTION | ix

PART ONE: The Model | 19
Chapter One: Anatomy of a Foodscape | 21
Chapter Two: Creating a Foodscape Framework: the Ornamentals | 31
Chapter Three: Just Add Edibles | 43
Chapter Four: What to Plant: Veggies & Herbs | 59
Chapter Five: What to Plant: Fruits, Nuts, Berries & Grains | 87
Chapter Six: Foodscape Basic Care & Maintenance | 103

PART TWO: Foodscaping Projects | 113
Foodie Fire Pit | 115
Property Screen Meadow | 123
Edible Neighborhood Entryway | 129
Patio Pots | 135
Alternative Growing Systems | 141

PART THREE: Yard to Table | 149
Harvesting, Preserving & Processing | 151
Recipes | 163
A Few Last Words | 171

✳

APPENDIX | 173
Ornamental Plants for Every Region | 175
Community Resources | 181
Index | 184
Acknowledgments | 187
About the Author | 189

INTRODUCTION

FOODSCAPING is the logical integration of edibles in a traditional ornamental landscape. In other words, to foodscape is to grow food alongside your flowers, within the landscape that already exists. It is a design and growing strategy that makes the most of the square footage in every landscape. I'm not suggesting everyone "become a farmer" by digging up the front yard – far from it. Through foodscaping, you can harness the sunny open mulch space that's already in a prime spot and add your favorite edibles like kale, tomatoes, peppers, eggplants, lettuce and carrots. The average suburban foundation landscape – the landscape around the house – offers open space the equivalent of 1,250 sq ft, or 48 average-sized 4x8 raised beds. That's a lot of edible potential! While an urban house on a small lot may offer less planting space, any sunny area can be foodscaped, even if you're living in a townhome or condo with only a deck or front porch.

Foundation landscapes should incorporate a beautiful mix of native ornamental plants, such as pink muhly grass and tender edibles like lemongrass.

In North Carolina where I live, builders cannot close on a new housing development without planning for developed space around each home, which means every homeowner (or renter) has a ready-made plot of land likely suitable for growing food, along with ornamental plants. This open space often has irrigation installed or, at the very least, is close to a water source. This is ideal for the foodscaper, since the closer to your home you can grow vegetables, the better you'll be able to care for them.

You might be asking, But what if I don't want to make a longterm commitment? That's the beauty of foodscaping: If life gets in the way one year and you didn't get those annual veggies in the ground, you don't have to worry about having an empty garden space for weeds to take over. You'll always have the shrubs, perennials and trees that were already there. Go ahead and enjoy them until you can get back to planting your edibles again.

"I'll Never Buy Lettuce Again"

My foodscaping story started when I was in college. Once a week I'd treat myself to lunch at the café down the street from the Horticulture building on campus. The café had the most delicious mac and cheese and pre-made salads. Unfortunately, one fateful day I got sick. Like, really sick. What I thought was the flu turned out to be E. coli from one of those salads. (Since then, I try to only eat lettuce I have grown, washed and prepared.)

Lettuce was my first "crop," and I grew it on my windowsill. A 99-cent investment provided enough seeds to grow and eat salad for six months. A few years into school, I moved out into "the country" with a group of fellow students. We lived on a hog farm and gardened in a plot the farmer had tilled for us. We wanted to grow completely organically

Fresh, organic lettuce grown in my foodscape is served year-round.

Homegrown lettuce in the setting sun

but we had absolutely no idea what we were doing. For one thing, we planted 300 cauliflowers but wouldn't treat them with anything chemical. (We didn't know that the natural pest control Bt, *Bacillus thuringiensis,* was perfectly legitimate and harmless.) Well, I cooked that cauliflower for hours and then made soup that was infested with cabbage worms! The sad part of that story is that here we were, going to school for horticulture, and all we were learning about was designing with and planting ornamentals – not about the wide, wide world of edible plants.

After my first cabbage worm experience as a young horticulture student, I've learned how to grow cruciferous vegetables without the extra "protein." This kohlrabi grows along a property border with colorful foliage edibles like Perilla and ornamental elephant ears (Colocasia esculentes 'Black Runner').

Beyond the Windowsill

I started foodscaping almost by accident, in 2005, when I bought my first home. I wanted to be able to access local organic produce, but I couldn't afford it. I didn't have the skills or tools to build raised beds, either. Instead, I started tucking my favorite food crops into the landscape beds that I had inherited. Inspired by Rosalind Creasy and her Edible Landscaping books, I set out to create a suburban yard that was both bountiful and beautiful despite my tight budget and concerns about my homeowners association's (HOA) covenants. Much to my surprise, a year into developing my first foodscape my garden was given the highest honor a suburban development can bestow upon a residence: Yard of the year! Though generally reserved for the artificially-managed green lawns and clipped-hedged sort of landscapes, my organic garden broke the mold. It was an empowering moment when I realized we can develop a balance between ornamentals and edibles *and* meet the landscape guidelines set by HOAs.

Eventually, my quarter-acre lot was bursting at the seams with a beautiful mix of turf, trees, flowering shrubs, perennials, and organic food such as soybeans, corn, squash and tomatoes. I started to dream about the massive potential the suburban landscape offers. Imagine if every house had a small foodscape that was professionally managed through the HOA fees? All residents would have access to fresh produce that would be just steps away from their home. When done right, foodscaping could allow people to have a lot more money to allocate to things other than food. Foodscaping is simply a

Make a bold statement by planting corn and zinnias together for increased pollinator activity.

way to strike a happy medium between the needs of homeowners (food) and the desires of the HOA (a tidy landscape).

I soon began thinking bigger: I saw that by utilizing the growing potential and open land of housing developments, businesses and school campuses, foodscaping could extend beyond the individual home and offer a solution for sustainable land management on a larger scale. Though urban farming is a sexy topic and a worthy one, the truth is that there are roughly 180 million acres devoted to suburban sprawl in the U.S. – that's more acreage than all of our national and state parks combined! I could visualize the untapped potential of what could be grown on under-utilized developed land like the suburban landscape. For example, many neighborhoods require that turf cover 80% of open land, with only 20% devoted to landscape. These percentages could be tweaked to better utilize the cultivated land for food development and ecosystem restoration. A win-win.

The ultimate aim of foodscape design is to make the most of the cultivated land while utilizing the existing shrub and turf base.

Over the past decade I have dedicated a lot of time to figuring out the dynamic between the woody ornamental plants that make up the average landscape, the turf space that manages excess water, and the vast square footage of open mulch space that immature landscapes offer. I gave myself a goal: to demonstrate in my own life how much food could be produced by integrating practical edibles into the common spaces of my own neighborhood. If it could work for me, then how could this design model potentially impact the accessibility of nutrition in every community? And for the landscape industry, which would naturally become involved, I asked: how does offering the service of growing food empower professionals for the future?

When I graduated from college, I went to work for a landscape company and managed their maintenance department. We spent a lot of time and resources on impractical land management strategies, like blowing the leaves away, only to replace them with mulch, which is, essentially, crumbled-up trees. We were taking away all of this great organic matter and spraying a ton of Roundup®. It was very frustrating for me. I kept thinking, *we come to these landscapes every week. We know how to take care of them, and the homeowners could be getting so much more value from their space because we have the knowledge to grow plants that would feed them and their community.*

Suburban landscapes have the potential to grow massive amounts of food. From serving the needs of the homeowners, to distributing to shelters, local restaurants and even school cafeterias – fresh, organic produce has a place in very community.

A summer foodscape of corn, okra, peppers, basil, marigolds, coleus, salvia and pennisetum.

The summer foodscape offers bounty and beauty.

The Bottom Line

Today, looking back on the foodscaping goal I set for myself ten years ago, I can see its effects in my own life, and they are substantial: the homegrown, organic lifestyle of my family has led me to cultivate a wide variety of edibles, including grains such as wheat and oats, and sugar sources such as cane sorghum. The foodscape provides so much abundance that we are able to grow 100% of certain foods, eliminating the need to ever purchase them. Garlic, onions, salad greens, peppers, peanuts and tomatoes are just a few examples. That makes a huge impact on my bank account and my peace of mind, knowing that I am eating food that was grown with an ethical standard.

Money isn't the only thing that's positively impacted by foodscaping; it also reduces food miles (the measurement of the fuel it takes to transport food from a distant farm to the consumer) and makes the landscape a more biodiverse habitat for insects, birds, butterflies, turtles, frogs and mammals. Right now, we as a culture place a large emphasis on gardening for wildlife and designing spaces for stormwater management, but we must also acknowledge that our landscapes should serve the needs of local communities. We can make that happen by growing nutritious edibles amongst our favorite ornamental specimens.

Looking Ahead

I am not under the illusion that suddenly homeowners everywhere will take the initiative to learn how to grow food. It is my goal, though, to make the foodscape model so mainstream that every landscape contractor offers it as a service. There are horticulture professionals who can cultivate food and flowers for you while managing your property in a sound and sustainable way. Most HOA landscapes are already professionally managed, so if the landscaper can also work with edibles, there's no additional cost to the homeowner. When landscapers adopt foodscaping, their businesses become more relevant because they're providing a vital service. However, change starts with individuals. Change will start with you — whether you're a homeowner or a landscaper.

It starts by getting people to associate landscapes with food production. I think of rice as a great "gateway plant." It looks just like the ornamental grasses we are used to growing — like fountain grass — and has much better structural integrity. While it's unlikely that you'll harvest enough rice in a foundation landscape to never need to purchase it, the meals you prepare from your homegrown plants will be special. This experience of eating what you've grown expands your awareness and appreciation of food. Even as a novelty, edibles deserve a place in the landscape to make people pay attention. There are okra plants that are as beautiful as hibiscus. People are already accustomed to seeing ornamental kale, cabbage and Swiss chard in the landscape. It's time to crank things up a notch.

There's a lot going on in this biodiverse, sustainable foodscape: Turf provides a permeable surface for water management. Flowers attract pollinators, while shrubs provide an architectural framework for the edibles.

Leading a Change

Once you make the switch in your mind to thinking about growing food in existing landscapes, every bit of open, sunny mulch space — school campuses, parks, office buildings, senior centers and new housing developments — will look like an opportunity just waiting to be cultivated.

This book will give you the tools to create your own foodscape and the information to work edibles into other landscapes you might manage beyond your home base, whether as a volunteer or as a paid contractor.

Benefits for homeowners

- Fresh food
- Reduced risk of food-borne illnesses
- Lower food costs
- Fewer pest problems in overall landscape (due to increased biodiversity)
- Decreased exposure to harmful chemicals in food
- Change of lifestyle with healthier food options
- Unexpected beauty
- The simple pleasure and fun of "doing it"

How foodscaping can change the world:

- Empowers individuals to learn/appreciate to grow food
- Increases local sustainable food production
- Reduces the food miles crisis
- Increases biodiversity in common landscapes
- Adds purpose to professional landscape installations

Come along with me as we enter into the wonderful world of Foodscaping. I hope you'll be inspired to dig in with me!

Brie

Part One:

THE MODEL

Learn the basics of transforming your landscape
into a foodscape with plant selection and tips
for design, maintenance and care.

One

ANATOMY OF A FOODSCAPE

A FOODSCAPE makes the most of the open square footage that exists in common landscapes around homes, buildings and parking lots. Residential landscapes, for example, offer many areas that are suitable for growing food. The space close around your home is known as the "foundation landscape." Frequently planted with easy-to-grow shrubs, a foundation landscape can go from ordinary to something that provides beauty, inspiration *and* delicious produce. As you move farther out from the foundation landscape, you will find other edible growing opportunities. Let's look at what's possible and desirable for these spaces: it's all about the zones!

It is important to consider what you want to grow and the best place to grow it since not all landscapes are created equal. Certain parts of the yard are better suited to growing, say, tomatoes, than other parts. As the garden maxim goes: "Right plant, right place." I look at foodscapes as having three growing zones, each based on its proximity to a house, ease of access and/or water sources. Let's face it – growing food will require some level of irrigation, and most people don't have a hose hookup out by the street. Additionally, you're more likely to harvest and use crops that are closer to your kitchen, i.e., growing in the areas that you pass by frequently. Near the house is the best place to grow things like herbs and salad greens so you can quickly run out and clip a handful for dinner.

The 3 Foodscape Growing Zones

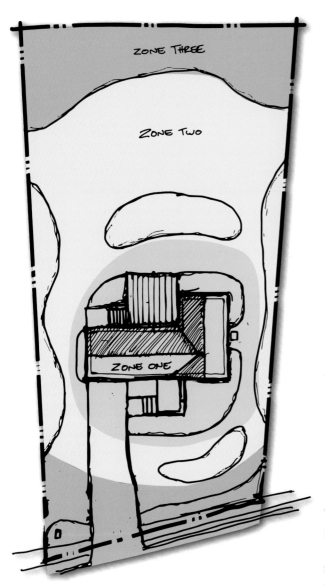

The foodscape zones proceed from the street to the house. In other words, they go from areas that receive the least amount of attention and care to areas that receive the most amount of attention and care. For the reasons I explain below, each zone will have a different ratio of edible plants to ornamentals:

- Foodscape Zone 3 (farthest from the house): 80% ornamentals to 20% edibles

- Foodscape Zone 2 (mid-yard): 60/40 ornamentals to edibles

- Foodscape Zone 1 (foundation landscape): 50/50 ornamentals to edibles

ZONE 3

Zone 3, farthest away from the house, is usually near the street and other property borders. It often has the least access to water and it can be the driest, unless that area of the yard is unusually soggy. Zone 3 garden beds near the street have more exposure to roadside pollutants from vehicle exhaust, roadside salt and chemicals.

You'll be providing care for the plants in Zone 3 less frequently – maybe once a week or less. In general, the landscape of Zone 3 is designed with ornamental plants, including trees, shrubs and perennials, leaving less room for seasonal edibles. However, this is a great place to site fruit trees such as persimmon and drought-tolerant fruiting shrubs like blackberries. When creating a foodscape in this area, 80% of the foodscape should be dedicated to ornamental plants, while 20% should be dedicated to edibles. Keep in mind that Zone 3 areas are front and center in the public eye, which is another reason to keep the most of the plantings as ornamental, just in case you don't plant seasonal edibles there every season.

It takes time to build up good soil fertility and structure in all parts of the foodscape, but because of its location, Zone 3 can be the last to receive attention, and so the soil is usually not as rich and fertile as soil in other areas of the yard – another reason to carefully select plants for this zone. You'll improve the soil in this area by planting-hole amendments (adding compost directly to the planting hole) and then mulching the entire bed. This will allow for weed suppression, water retention and tidiness. You don't need to add a thick layer of compost to an entire bed before you plant and then mulch again on top. After planting, if you mulch yearly, the soil will continue to improve as the mulch breaks down.

Because of the lower soil fertility and lower time spent caring for plants in Zone 3, all seasonal annual edibles and flowers should be direct-sown – planted as seeds directly into the garden. (Learn more about planting edibles in Chapter Three.) Direct-sown plants establish much deeper and more extensive root systems, so they're considerably more drought tolerant than transplants. For new trees and shrubs, keep a close eye for several weeks and water frequently after you first plant them – every day at first, then

moving to every other day, a couple times a week, and weekly. Eventually, they'll need no supplemental water unless your geographical area is experiencing a prolonged drought, but everything does need to be watered thoroughly and frequently immediately after being planted.

Trees & Shrubs

- Apple
- Blackberry
- Cherry
- Chestnut
- Fig
- Honeyberry
- Paw Paw
- Peach
- Pecan
- Persimmon
- Raspberry
- Walnut

Seasonal Annual Edibles & Flowers

Warm Season

- Amaranth
- Celosia
- Dry Corn *(such as Bloody Butcher, an heirloom variety)*
- Mexican Sunflower
- Peanut
- Sorghum
- Soybean
- Sweet Corn
- Zinnia

Cool Season

- Carrot
- Collards
- Horseradish
- Mustard Greens
- Parsnip
- Rhubarb
- Rutabaga
- Turnip

ZONE 2

Zone 2 is between the street and the house: mid-yard. This could be an island flower bed in the front or back yard or a landscape bed delineating the property lot line. Zone 2 areas usually have better access to water than Zone 3 but still may not get watered as frequently as plantings closer to the house. Unless you have a sprinkler system on a timer, it can take a bit more effort to water these areas (i.e., dragging hoses and watering cans around).

I manage Zone 2 by planting only twice a year. This is where my grain meadows (with inter-planted herbs and flowers) grow. It's possibly one of the most low-maintenance ways to garden, and it looks attractive. As a bonus, the edible meadow acts to screen the view from the street and provides seasonal privacy. Zone 2 areas are usually planted with a ratio of 60% ornamentals to 40% edibles, leaving enough ornamental interest to keep the bed looking full year-round, no matter what stage of growth the edibles are in. (See page 123 for how to create a property screen meadow.)

It's important to spend more time prepping the soil in Zone 2. I recommend spreading between 3-5" of compost seasonally before planting, then finishing the beds with mulch. The soil will gradually build fertility over time, but will do so faster than soil in Zone 3 areas because of the yearly broad application of compost. This is still an area where the bulk of edibles and flowers should be direct-sown to give you lower maintenance.

Trees & Shrubs

- Aronia
- Currant
- Blackberry
- Dwarf Fruit Trees
- Elderberry
- Hazelnut (Filbert)
- Honeyberry
- Gooseberry
- Grape
- Raspberry

Seasonal Annual Edibles & Flowers

Warm Season

- Basil
- Buckwheat
- Chive
- Celosia
- Cleome
- Coleus
- Cosmos
- Eggplant
- Peanut
- Pepper
- Sesame
- Soybean
- Strawflower
- Sunflower
- Sweet Corn
- Sweet Potato
- Tomatillo
- Zinnia

Cool Season

- Alyssum
- Beet
- Carrot
- Cilantro
- Cornflower
- Dill
- Garlic
- Swiss Chard
- Kale
- Larkspur
- Leek
- Lettuce
- Oats
- Onion
- Parsnip
- Poppy
- Potato
- Rhubarb
- Snapdragon
- Turnip
- Wheat

ZONE 1

Zone 1 is the foundation landscape right around the house. This space touches the house or sidewalk leading to the front door. If you're working with a traditional foundation landscape that has been installed by a developer, there will already be a 50/50 balance of ornamental plants and open mulch space. Everyone with a newly-built house has a Zone 1 landscape area. Patio home and townhome dwellers pretty much only have Zone 1 landscapes. (Pots and alternative growing systems require enough attention that they're also considered to be in Zone 1.)

Zone 1 is where you'll grow your everyday edibles – things that you cook with frequently. Plant tons of greens, particularly lettuce and basil, along

Malabar spinach

with peppers, tomatoes, cucumbers and plants that need a lot of water in this zone. This is also a great place to grow hydroponic tomatoes (see page 141). During the winter, I grow onions and garlic as the bed edges in these spaces. Summer squash works particularly well as a groundcover because you can easily check the plants and harvest before fruits are too big to eat. I like to grow Malabar spinach along the front porch for privacy and greenery. If you need support structures for any of the plants in this area, you can make use of patio railings that are already attached to your home.

Amend the soil in Zone 1 as you would in Zone 2. Spread 6" of compost on top of the existing soil, taking care not to create "volcanoes" or "bathtubs" around trees and shrubs. This is where you'll grow your most finicky and sensitive crops, so it's where you'll want to have the best soil. Learn more about preparing the soil and planting in Chapters 2 and 3.

PLANTS FOR ZONE 1

You can grow pretty much everything in Zone 1, including all plants listed in Zones 2 and 3, as well as the following seasonal annual edibles.

Warm Season
- Cucumber
- Rice
- Squash – summer and winter
- Tomato

Cool Season
- Arugula
- Chive
- Lettuce

Mixed lettuce

Creating New Planting Beds in Zones 2 and 3

Since Zone 1 landscapes will have already been established by the developer, the rest of the available land will likely just be lawn, if there is anything at all. Rarely will a new house have garden beds in Zones 2 or 3. You, as the homeowner, will have to decide if you want to install those for property screens and privacy.

When establishing new foodscape beds where there is existing lawn, you must remove the sod, otherwise known as lawn (if you're planning to extend the landscape beds in Zone 1 out into Zone 2, you'll also want to remove the sod). Don't be fooled by the technique of laying cardboard on top of the sod and hoping to smother everything underneath. This does not work! For those of us living in warm climates with spreading turfs like centipedegrass and Bermuda grass, it is critical to completely remove the sod, or you will be fighting it for the rest of your life.

Use the right tool to make the task efficient. Rent a sod cutter or hire a landscape professional; it's worth it. I also recommend consulting a designer for guidance on bed expansion so that your foodscape is proportional, attractive, meets the legal requirements of your HOA covenants and, most importantly, so that you don't bite off more than you can chew and end up getting discouraged before you even start on the edibles.

Once the sod has been removed, layer compost on top of the bare earth, also considered the natural grade of the land. Spread compost to a

depth of 6"-8". Then, rake the compost around to come up to the grade of the trees and shrubs, again taking care not to create a bathtub depression where water will stand. You can layer this compost on top of the soil and not till it in, as the earthworms will do the work of incorporating the new soil into the old, over time. Soil preparation is the single most important step of building a foodscape. Every bit of time and money you put into building great soil will come back to you in a bountiful harvest and reduced work to get it.

Finish beds using the mulch of your choice – but never use anything made of rubber. I love triple-shredded hardwood mulch and ground leaves because they help retain moisture, suppress weeds, break down quickly and add organic matter to the soil.

Now that you understand the zones of a foodscape, you're ready to plant or enhance an existing framework of ornamentals.

Two

Creating a Foodscape Framework:
The Ornamentals

TO HAVE A FOODSCAPE, you have to have an ornamental plant framework. The area closely surrounding your home is known as the foundation landscape. You probably already have a good balance of ornamental plantings and open space. So why even talk about adding ornamental (mostly non-edible) plants since I keep telling you that this is simple and that you don't have to start over? In case you're apprehensive, I promise this isn't a bait-and-switch.

It's possible that the foundation landscape around your house is thin or that you think the plants are ugly. Maybe they're old and overgrown and you want to start fresh, or maybe they're young and boring. Perhaps you'd just like to add more evergreens for year-round interest or to provide a better backdrop for your edibles. Your rainbow chard will look better growing in front of a boxwood than in front of nothing at all.

The important thing is to find a balance between ornamentals and edibles. Ornamentals, oddly enough, are the most critical part of the foodscape, as they are the permanent features that add color, texture and biodiversity. If your entire landscape were all food, you wouldn't know where to begin and you would be overwhelmed by having to replace everything seasonally.

Peanuts growing in a formal landscape.

Design Styles

No matter the style of garden you prefer – from English cottage garden to minimalist – there are beautiful ways to integrate food into it. In new developments particularly, you will primarily be dealing with a young and underdeveloped formal design. Almost every house will have a base layer of permanent evergreen shrubs that will eventually grow together (that's how people in older houses ended up with monster yew hedges out front that require a backhoe to remove). A newer landscape is one of the easiest to start with in terms of adding food because there's still plenty of open space and sunshine.

Assessing and Improving the Ornamental Landscape

If you inherited a landscape full of plants you don't like, creating a foodscape gives you the opportunity to start anew. If, on the other hand, you're fine with the ornamentals already in place but want to make the landscape more functional, simply start by improving on what you inherited.

The first thing I do as a designer is to add biodiversity through the ornamental plant collection. The developer-planted landscapes I see where I live include a lot of plants in the holly family, so I start by adding in different families of plants. By increasing biodiversity, you're encouraging the arrival of more beneficial insects and pollinators, which, in the long run, benefits the edibles. Some of my go-to plants for a Southern foodscape include Encore® azaleas, Knock Out® roses, butterfly bushes, hydrangeas, quince and fall and spring blooming camellias. I also like to incorporate native plants such as *Fothergilla* and *Itea* which have beautiful fall foliage and flowers that provide nectar seasonally. The most important part of being a designer is to understand and meet the needs of my client. I want to know what the goals of each unique the foodscape are – what colors, textures and seasons do my clients want to experience? It's important to me to ask what they like – if they're happier with pink flowers, or blue, or if they want landscape interest during a particular season.

If you're confused about the plants in your foundation landscape, find a reputable landscape designer in your area and get some feedback about how large they're likely to grow, when they'll bloom (or not), whether they're evergreen, and if they have any special soil requirements. For example, azaleas grow best in slightly acidic soil, which is not necessarily optimal for cabbage family plants. Also, if you know the name of a plant, there are many online sites where you can find advice.

Emphasis on Trees and Shrubs

Foodscaping focuses on two main plant groups because they are relatively easy to grow: 1) ornamental trees and shrubs, and 2) seasonal annuals (a mix of flowers and edibles). Trees and shrubs go in the ground and go to town. A bit of pruning for structure every now and then and a

seasonal hit of organic fertilizer and they're good to go. You plant annuals each season, reap the benefits, and then yank them out. If you've grown a petunia, you can grow lettuce; they're both seasonal annuals.

'Limelight' hydrangea makes a good backdrop for a basil edge.

A third plant group, perennials, can be more challenging to deal with because you find yourself struggling with these common questions: When should I cut back? When should I divide them? How do I plant perennials to make sure there's something pretty and colorful blooming all of the time?

In my experience as a home gardener I find it easier to start a design with woody ornamentals, such as trees and shrubs, that don't disappear underground in winter and will retain a year-round structure in the garden – and then think about incorporating flowering plants that add color and texture. I have become very selective about the perennial plants that I grow as some varieties can spread vigorously or reseed, taking up space that I'd rather devote to growing food.

It ultimately comes down to what garden maintenance tasks do you enjoy? I don't like digging and dividing; I prefer sowing seed and replanting each season. There's no harm in adding well-behaved perennials but don't beat yourself up if you choose to stick to lower-maintenance plants in your foodscape. Give yourself permission to make the most out of your landscape on your terms.

Plant Types: A Few Examples

Woody Ornamentals (plants that keep their woody structure and don't die back to the ground in winter)

- Azalea
- Hydrangea
- Crape Myrtle
- Camellia
- Yew

Perennials (plants that die to the ground in fall and winter, but keep their rootstock and come back in the spring for two or more years)

- Agastache
- Black-Eyed Susan
- Penstemon
- Purple Coneflower
- Sedum 'Autumn Joy'

Purple coneflower

Colorful & Dependable Annual Flowers for Your Foodscape

If you'd like to add annual flowers to your foodscape, here are some good options. They're easy to grow from seed most anywhere and pack a punch with pollinators.

Cuphea

Melampodium

Warm Season Annuals

I find that my summer plant palette has more flowering annuals than edibles because of where I live; my options for food crops that I can grow in the heat of the Carolina summer are a bit slim. If you live in a cooler region, you might have more edibles overlapping seasons than I do.

- Callibrochoa
- Celosia
- Coleus
- Cuphea
- Lantana
- Marigold
- Melampodium *(it reseeds, but is easy to pull out)*
- Perilla *(pull it out before it goes to seed)*
- Salvia, annual varieties
- Zinnia

Cool Season Annuals

- Alyssum
- Calendula
- Ornamental Kale and Cabbage
- Petunia
- Snapdragon
- Viola

Cactus-flower zinnia

Fruit & Nut Trees in the Ornamental Framework

I don't bother much with fruit trees. They require so much work in order to get them to produce edible fruit, and there are lots of great organic options at the grocery and farmers' markets for staples like apples, peaches and pears. Of course, there's nothing stopping you from growing fruit trees, but I find the time, energy and money required to get a substantial harvest is not worth it. I *will*, however, plant some native trees that produce hard-to-find fruits that don't ship well. Persimmons and paw paws are wonderful options because they're easy. Instead of an ornamental pear (please never plant one of those), try a paw paw; they're on the smaller side and they produce delicious fruits!

As for nut-bearing trees, if you have room for larger shade trees, plant a pecan or chestnut, but be sure to position it on the north side of the bed so it doesn't steal sunlight from your other edible plants. Almond and hazelnut are slightly smaller and can be inter-planted with the shrubs and seasonal edibles.

Plants for Your Region

Important note: As you've seen, I have been using my North Carolina foodscape as a template and I have mentioned a few of my favorite ornamental plants — some of which may not do as well in other parts of North America. And there are lots of plants that I can't grow successfully that do beautifully elsewhere. If you'd like some plant selection advice for your area, please visit the extensive plant-list section at the back of the book, "Ornamentals for Every Region." It can help give you some inspiration in designing your foodscape framework.

Planting the Ornamental Framework: Trees and Shrubs

The next chapter will focus mostly on planting the seasonal edibles, and the techniques and issues specific to them. But first, here's your crash course on planting trees and shrubs.

Prepare the Soil

Whenever you're about to embark on a big gardening project, it's a good idea to have your soil tested. That way, you'll know exactly what you're working with. What's in the soil (or not in the soil), in addition to the soil pH and structure, has a huge impact on plant health. If you  do end up needing to make some adjustments to the soil, better to do that as you're planning.

To test your soil, download the necessary instructions and forms from your local Cooperative Extension office. Extension services originate from land grant universities such as Purdue University (my alma matter) or NC State, near my house. They have offices throughout each state, regardless of where the "mothership" university is. You can look up information about soil testing and download forms from the website for your state's extension agency. All you'll have to do is mail in or drop off the soil sample. You'll get a report via mail or email.

The next chapter will focus mostly on planting the

Interpreting a Soil Test

The soil test will give you some specific information to act upon. Test results will tell you about certain qualities of the soil, including:

- Soil pH
- Soil class (mineral, mineral organic, organic)
- Humic matter percentage
- CEC (Cation Exchange Capacity)
- Macro nutrients: levels of nitrogen (N), phosphorus (P) and potassium (K).
- Micro nutrients: including, but not limited to, levels of magnesium, copper, sulfur and calcium

These numbers, and the way the soil characteristics they indicate interact, will lead to the more important (for gardeners) parts of the soil test, which are the lime and fertilizer recommendations compiled from an analysis of the data contained in the soil test.

These recommendations will be listed in pounds per 1,000 square feet of surface area. Multiply the length times the width of the garden area to see how many square feet you need to cover. Doing this will help you determine how much lime or fertilizer to purchase.

You may read here and there that if your soil has a low pH, you should add lime, and if your soil has a high pH, you should add sulfur, but the pH number itself doesn't tell the whole story. It also doesn't give you specific information about what to add and how much, which is why the recommendations in the soil test are important.

I don't want you to freak out, though. If you were planning on gardening without much math, you can – for the most part. If you start noticing weirdly-colored leaves or plants that aren't producing fruit, it is possible that the problem is in the soil and it's something that can be corrected with the right information. So, why not start with the right information and try to head off a few issues before they appear?

Once you have the soil test results, you can prepare the soil. I recommend starting by adding compost to the top of all beds where you'll be growing edibles. Spread compost to a depth of 4-6 inches. Here's where you have to do more math (sorry!).

To figure out how much compost to buy, multiply the length of the bed (in feet) by the width of the bed (in feet). If you have a 4x10 bed, that's 40 square feet. Compost and mulch is, however, sold in cubic yards. To calculate the number of yards you need, follow this formula: multiply bed square feet x inches of compost depth x 0.0031. This will give you the number of cubic yards needed. For example, for 5 inches of mulch, you would need .62 cubic yards (that's 40 square feet times 5 inches times 0.0031).

You do not have to till or dig the compost into the planting bed. The earthworms will take care of incorporating it. If you're planting closer to the street in foodscape Zone 3 (see page 22 and next page), you can mulch just around the plants, instead of spreading it across the entire bed.

If you need to incorporate lime or fertilizer, now is the time to do it. Sprinkle it over the compost and rake it in to mix it a bit. These amendments may need to be added yearly, but also get a soil test *before* adding ingredients that will influence the pH reading.

Decide on Plant Placement & Spacing

When creating a new foodscape bed from scratch, remember to factor in the eventual mature size of any trees or shrubs you plant, including the shade that will be cast by the tree canopies. Because most edibles need full sun, you will likely be planting more edibles when you first install a new bed than you will 10 years down the line. If you don't want to, or can't, fill in all the space in your new bed at first, don't worry. It will just look immature landscape, and there's nothing wrong with that.

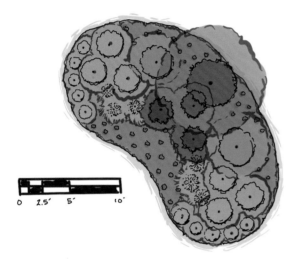

0   2.5'   5'   10'

Draw a simple diagram to help you determine how many plants to plant. Make a scale that correlates inches to feet and draw circles for the trees and shrubs you're planting. The smaller circles will be the size the plant is when it goes into the ground. The larger circles will indicate the eventual size of the mature plant, including the shade of the tree canopy. To learn the expected mature sizes of trees and shrubs, read the plant tags or research the plants online (it never hurts to do a little bit of advanced planning prior to going shopping!).

Note: As you plan your new bed, be sure to review the ratio of ornamentals to edibles for each of the three foodscape zones, on page 22.

Keep these ratios in mind when planning and planting:

Foodscape Zone 3 (farthest from the house): 80% ornamentals to 20% edibles

Foodscape Zone 2 (mid-yard): 60/40 ornamentals to edibles

Foodscape Zone 1 (foundation landscape): 50/50 ornamentals to edibles

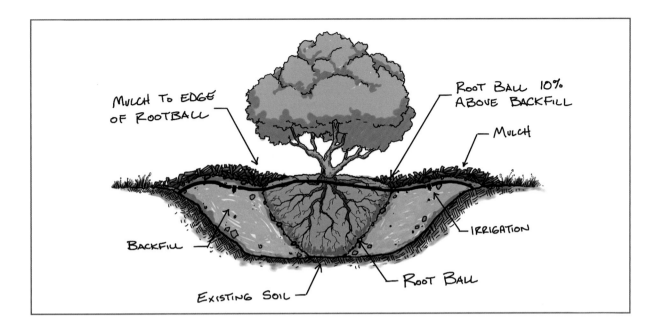

Labels on diagram:
MULCH TO EDGE OF ROOTBALL
ROOT BALL 10% ABOVE BACKFILL
MULCH
IRRIGATION
BACKFILL
EXISTING SOIL
ROOT BALL

Follow These Planting Tips

Planting trees and shrubs is easy! Follow these four steps and use this image as reference.

1. Dig the planting holes for trees and shrubs so they are twice as wide as the root ball and slightly less deep.

2. Remove the plant from its containers and test the planting hole depth. If the top of the root ball is below soil grade, add some backfill to the hole, press it down, and check the depth again.

3. Fill the planting hole with the same soil you removed. Do not mix in compost or soil amendments.

4. Mulch with compost and/or shredded hardwood mulch, taking care not to make a mulch volcano around the three or shrub. You really don't want the mulch to touch the stem or trunk.

Water daily to establish the plant, counting to ten while directing the water at the root ball of each plant. You can gradually cut back watering to every other day, every few days, once a week, and then only if there isn't rain for two or three weeks. I'd like to give you a foolproof watering plan, but it really does depend on the weather and how fast the plant grows roots. You never want the soil to be soggy and muddy for extended periods of time, but it should not be allowed to completely dry out for the first several weeks after planting.

Finishing Up

Edging the landscape bed gives it a nice, tidy look (popular with HOAs). You absolutely do not have to cut an edge in all of the beds, and you definitely don't have to do it every week. However, water and mulch stay nicely contained in edged beds (a heavy rain can create a mulch river if there's no edge to catch the mulch). You can rent a power edger once a year, hire a landscaper to edge, or you can cut an edge the old-fashioned way: with a shovel. If you choose to go that route, stand facing the bed with a flat-edge shovel. Push the shovel in at an angle and cut the sod so that the edge of the landscape bed slopes toward you.

Wine bottle edge created with leftovers from my frequent dinner parties.

I like to edge my foodscape beds in the back yard with wine bottles. You can create a single row of bottles stuck into the ground or build bottle "walls." These walls will add up to five degrees of heat to the soil during the winter, which allows me to grow heading vegetables such as broccoli, cauliflower and cabbage without cover during the colder months of the year.

After you've edged the beds, spread a 2-3" layer of shredded hardwood bark mulch to help retain moisture, suppress weeds, and make it "pretty."

Once the foodscape framework is planted, you're ready for the fun part: adding edibles!

Three

Just Add Edibles

NOW THAT YOU'VE GOT an ornamental framework of evergreen trees, shrubs, flowering perennials and ornamental grasses, you can get to the good stuff: planting veggies, herbs, fruits, nuts and grains! Almost every type of edible can find a home in the landscape somewhere, but some plants are better suited for certain locations than others. In the garden, half the battle is planting the right plant in the right place. The other half is planting the right plant at the right time.

Seasonal Shuffle

I tend to grow a lot of seasonal annual vegetables and herbs because that's what makes up the bulk of our diet. Sure, rhubarb is a perennial edible and will be there for you next year, but really, how much rhubarb can one person eat? I'm much more interested in selecting a few plant types and growing as much as I can of each of those foods so that I make a measurable dent in my grocery bill and my food miles.

Gardeners who live in areas with cool summer nights can grow a wider variety of edibles at the same time. Pictured here: tomato, eggplant, kale, dill, kale.

Red leaf lettuce snuggled up with some hellebores. They are both at their best in my garden during the cool season.

Just as the name would suggest, seasonal edibles each have their time to shine. Some grow best during cooler months (cool season), which could be winter or could be early spring or late fall, depending on where you live. Others grow best during the heat of summer (warm season). Unless you garden in an area that has cool nights all summer (certain parts of the Northwest, Northern Plains and Northeast), you'll likely switch out your edible plantings at least once per year in a big seasonal swap. In cooler regions, you can grow many edibles at the same time, but you have to give a little extra help (which I'll explain) to heat lovers such as tomatoes and peppers.

Because "right plant at the right time" is so important, I want to take some time to talk about growing food in the landscape in terms of seasons and temperature requirements, to give you all of the basic information you need to help you be a successful gardener.

Plants respond to temperatures and day length, both of which are influenced by the seasons. If, for example, you try to grow a plant like lettuce, which flowers during long days (typically in the summertime), you'll have trouble with bolting (flowering) because you want to eat the leaves and not the flowers. So you have to grow lettuce during "short day" times (spring and fall). Tomatoes and peppers are "day neutral." They'll flower regardless of day length, which is good because you need flowers in order to get fruit; however, these plants simply will not grow when soil and air temperatures are too low, which is why it's hard to get tomatoes (for example) to grow in areas with cool nights during the summer and why the plants will just sit in the garden and not grow if you plant them too early in the spring. Temperature is the limiting factor for tomatoes and many other plants.

Edible meadow during the summer (corn, sorghum, sunflowers, zinnias).

Location, Location, Location!

Plant basil as an edible border and you'll always have plenty to eat fresh, freeze, make pesto, and give away.

Matching the plant to the place is the key to efficiently using your space and available sunlight to grow the maximum amount of food.

I've compiled a list of some of the places where you can pop edible plants into the landscape and the plants that will thrive in those locations.

Edible Edges

Hands-down, the easiest way to incorporate edibles into your foundation landscape is along the edges. This is where the sun is usually most plentiful and it's an area that is easy to reach for planting, watering and harvesting. These are my go-to edging edibles.

Cool Season

- **Garlic**
- **Greens** (including arugula, lettuce, mustard)
- **Onion**
- **Parsley**
- **Potato**

Warm Season

- **Basil**
- **Bush beans**
- **Peanuts**
- **Pepper**
- **Soybean**

Groundcovers

Vining plants make perfect groundcovers, as do some self-sowing greens. I particularly like to plant squash and pumpkins as summer groundcovers. When they start to look tired, pull them up! There is no reason to be a vegetable-growing martyr. We're talking about foodscaping, so we want everything to look nice. If a plant isn't meeting your aesthetic needs, yank it out.

Cool Season

- Arugula
- Kale
- Lettuce
- Mustard
- Strawberries

Warm Season

- Cucumber
- Pumpkin (if you have a lot of space)
- Squash
- Sweet Potato

Pumpkin growing as a groundcover

Arugula makes a great groundcover.

Co-Op Plants

Panicle hydrangeas provide sturdy support for large tomato plants.

These are the edible plants that need some sort of support and grow best when they can climb, sprawl and twine up through another plant. Deciduous flowering shrubs such as spirea, viburnum, hydrangea and lilacs – common plants with good structural integrity – can handle the amount of biomass that an heirloom tomato creates. You wouldn't even know a tomato is climbing through it.

Cool Season

- Peas

Warm Season

- Cucumber & Squash *(might need some help to climb)*
- Pole Bean
- Tomato

Beauty Queens

A successful foodscape is as beautiful as it is functional. These plants are garden standouts, but also blend well to create a mosaic of color in the landscape alongside ornamental counterparts.

If you like ornamental grass, you'll love:

- Corn
- Oats
- Rice
- Sorghum
- Wheat

If you like flowering kale, you'll love:

- Arugula
- Broccoli
- Cauliflower
- Kale
- Lettuce

If you like coleus you'll love:

- Basil
  (purple-leafed variety)
- Mustard Greens
- Swiss Chard

Instead of small shrubs and perennials plant:

- Basil
- Bush Beans
- Eggplant
- Pepper
- Soybean
- Tomatillo

Peppers are right at home in this mixed border of flowers, shrubs and vines next to the hidden water garden.

Planting Seasonal Annual Edibles & Flowers

The way you plant seasonal annual edibles and flowers is crucial to their success. Whenever possible, I like to direct sow edibles (plant seeds right into the garden) because direct sown plants are much more drought tolerant, and therefore need less attention and maintenance than transplanted plants. When you're growing a lot of edibles, every bit of time saved is important! These are my tips for planting seasonal edibles so that you can harvest bountiful crops.

What to Plant, When

Set yourself up for success by planting the right plants at the right time.

Cool Season

- Artichoke
- Arugula
- Asparagus *(perennial)*
- Artichoke
- Beet
- Broccoli
- Brussels Sprouts
- Carrot
- Cauliflower
- Celery
- Cilantro
- Collards
- Fennel
- Garlic
- Kale
- Lettuce
- Mizuna
- Mustard Greens
- Oats
- Onion
- Bok Choy, Pak Choi
- Parsley
- Pea
- Potato
- Radish
- Rhubarb *(perennial)*
- Scallions
- Shallots
- Spinach
- Swiss Chard
- Turnip
- Wheat

Warm Season

- Amaranth
- Corn
- Cucumber
- Eggplant
- Peanut
- Pepper
- Rice
- Sorghum
- Soybean
- Summer Squash
- Sunflower
- Sweet Potato
- Tomato
- Watermelon *(and melons)*
- Winter Squash *(and pumpkins)*

I talk about soil prep a lot, but that is because it is the single most important factor in your foodscaping success. The soil is the "base of operations" for plants, where they'll get everything they need – minerals, water, nutrients and oxygen.

Every time I plant edibles, I spread a 3-6" layer of compost on top of the previous season's mulch. That's it! For all the talk, soil prep is pretty simple! This presupposes, though, that you got a soil test when planning the foodscape framework and you know if your soil has any major deficiencies or issues that need to be addressed. Also, avoid walking on the nice, fluffy compost that you've spread, as foot traffic will compact it and impact the soil's ability to drain.

You can buy compost by the cubic yard and have it delivered, or you can buy bagged compost. For as much as you'll use in the foodscape, I recommend finding a good source and having it delivered.

Planting: Direct Sowing

"Direct sowing" means planting seeds directly into the garden instead of in flats indoors. Whenever possible, I advocate for direct sowing because plants can literally hit the ground running and their roots are never disturbed by moving them out of a flat. In the foodscape Zone 3 (farthest out from the house), all edibles need to be direct-sown. In Zones 1 and 2 (closer in), direct sowing will cut down drastically on initial and ongoing maintenance.

Almost every edible will grow well when direct sown, but it's important to note that the seeds that are most difficult to sow directly are those that take a long time to germinate. The issue that you might run into is a growing season that's not long enough for a plant that's been direct sown to reach maturity, which is why it's often recommended to sow, say, tomatoes and peppers indoors and then transplant them into the garden. However, you can direct sow tomatoes, but keep in mind that you will have to thin them to a single plant, as they will not perform in crowded growing conditions. Celery and other "heading" vegetables like cabbage, broccoli and cauliflower also need space to develop and grow best when transplanted with proper spacing.

Sowing Methods

When you think of direct sowing, you might immediately think of scattering seeds like chicken feed. That is one method – and you do use it to plant an edible meadow – but that's not the only way. Additionally, even if you scatter seeds, you can plan and organize where you're sowing them.

Grains can be direct sown in clumps to mimic the look of an ornamental grass.

Larkspur and poppies are gorgeous additions to the foodscape.

Broadcast sowing

I broadcast sow most plants in the edible meadow, edible neighborhood entryway, and in the non-edging edibles in foodscape Zone 3. I also broadcast sow zinnias and other seasonal flowers, some greens, and herbs such as cilantro and dill. The desired effect of this sowing method is to create a more natural looking landscape where colors and textures mingle, like a native meadow. This approach can be utilized even in formal designs, by mixing seeds in open areas that are surrounded by sheared hedges, like boxwoods and yews. It is also a very easy, low-maintenance approach to covering large areas of space. I plant one type of plant at a time, even if I'm mixing them together, rather than clumping plant types, so that I can achieve the density I want of seeds sown. I'll sow grains first, like wheat and oats, and gently rake them into the soil to provide some soil covereage. Then I will surface-sow seeds of cilantro, carrots and cool-season flowers like poppies and larkspur. These small seeds germinate best with exposure to light, therefore I do not cover them with soil or mulch at the time of sowing.

Stand on the outside of the bed while you're broadcast sowing so you don't compress the soil and so that your shoes don't pick up seeds that you've just sown.

Grab a handful of seeds and fling them away from you as if you're scattering chicken feed. If you've marked planting areas, try to contain the seed drop area to the marks, but don't worry if the lines get a little blurred. Spacing and density depend on the plants. Here are some good candidates for direct sowing:

- Amaranth
- Arugula
- Carrot
- Cilantro
- Lettuce
- Mizuna
- Mustard Greens
- Oats
- Rice
- Wheat

After planting, cover seeds with 3" of mulch. There are a few types of seeds that you don't want to cover: poppies, larkspur, love-in-a-mist, and arugula do well without being covered. A good rule of thumb is that the larger the seed, the more it needs to be covered. Dust-like seeds do not need to be covered.

Thumbing-in Seeds

There are several places where I mention "thumbing-in seeds." This is just what it sounds like: place a seed on top of the soil and use your thumb to press it a 1/2-1" into the soil. (The bigger the seed, the farther down into the soil it can be placed.)

Planting this way allows you to control spacing better for plants that grow larger and wider than the plants you are broadcast sowing. Good candidates for thumbing-in include:

- Corn
- Cucumber
- Garlic
- Peanut
- Soybean
- Summer Squash
- Sunflower
- Watermelon
  (and melons)
- Winter Squash
  (and pumpkin)

Thumbing-in seeds is exactly as it sounds!

Planting in Trenches or Rows

Edging plants are easy to plant in trenches. Use a shovel, soil knife or hand hoe to dig a shallow trench along the edge of the bed. (The depth depends on the plant.) Then place seeds at desired spacing and cover. This is a little quicker than "thumbing" and useful if you're planting in a row. (The row doesn't have to be straight; it can be a curve following the edge of a landscape bed.) You can plant anything you can "thumb" in trenches, but trenches are best for plants that are going to be somewhat close together. Squash and cucumbers aren't great for trenches because you don't need 20 plants in a 10-foot row.

Plants ideal for trenches:

- Arugula
- Asparagus (perennial)
- Beet
- Carrot
- Cilantro
- Collards
- Garlic
- Kale
- Lettuce
- Mizuna
- Mustard Greens
- Onion
- Parsnip
- Pea
- Potato
- Radish
- Scallions
- Shallots
- Spinach
- Swiss Chard
- Turnip

Warm Season

- Amaranth
- Corn
- Eggplant
- Peanut
- Rice
- Sorghum
- Soybean
- Sunflower
- Sweet Potato

Potatoes, garlic and onions are good candidates for trench planting because you're not technically planting "transplants," you're planting slips or bulbs, which function like big seeds.

A handheld hoe makes quick work of trench planting

Growing Transplants

High-dollar plants – plants with expensive seed or fruits and vegetables you covet – are best when grown from transplants. Tomatoes, for example, can cost $5 for 15 seeds if you're growing a fancy or rare variety. Plants that take a long time to germinate are good to grow from seed in the greenhouse or on the windowsill because it's easier to keep an eye on them there and keep them watered until they germinate. Plant transplants for edibles that require wider spacing than the flowers and grains. That way you won't waste time thinning or waste seeds (from thinning). If you do have to thin, most young seedlings are perfectly edible and can be thrown in salads. But, do not eat seedlings of plants in the nightshade family – tomatoes, eggplants, peppers, potato. They are poisonous. Stick with eating thinned seedlings of salad greens and root vegetables, except for potato.

It's easier to grow some cool season vegetables as transplants for spring planting than it is to direct sow them. Cool soil temperatures in spring provide an ideal breeding ground for soil-borne diseases, which can cause seeds to rot. Transplants can usually handle the cooler soil. Here's what and when to grow from transplants.

Cool Season Vegetable Transplants for Spring Planting

- Broccoli
- Cauliflower
- Celery
- Collards
- Fennel
- Kale
- Mizuna
- Oats
- Bok Choy, Pak Choi,
- Parsley
- Scallions
- Shallots
- Spinach
- Swiss Chard
- Wheat

Warm Season

- Corn
- Eggplant
- Pepper
- Tomato

Communal Flats

Certain plants do well when sown in "communal flats" and planted out into the garden in clumps. If you want to grow grains that look more like ornamental grass clumps than a wider meadow, communal flats are a good way to do this. They are like big "pans" for growing plants. They don't have cellpack dividers. You can sow seeds in the flats and then cut out "chunks" to plant in the landscape. Plants that do well in communal flats include:

- Kale
- Lettuce
- Oats
- Rice
- Swiss Chard
- Wheat

Hardening-off

Anything grown as a transplant needs to be hardened-off before planting outside. Hardening-off is simply the process of helping plants get used to outdoor conditions when they've started their lives growing indoors. You'll harden-off plants for cool weather and warm weather planting. Start by placing plants in an outdoor covered or protected area (such as a porch) for the day. Bring them inside at night. After a few days, leave the plants outside day and night. Within the week, you can plant them out into the garden.

The next two chapters feature my favorite edible plants with helpful information and growing tips for each one. I have not provided an exhaustive list of spacing, seasonal information or timing. My purpose is simply to get you going in the right direction so that you can take it from there.

Four

WHAT TO PLANT:
Veggies & Herbs

I CAN'T WRITE A GARDENING BOOK without touching on particular requirements, growing tips, ideas for cooking, and oddities of the plants you're most likely to sow in your foodscape. In this chapter and the next, unless I mention something different in the plant descriptions, assume that all of these edibles need to be planted in full sun in medium-moist, well-drained soil. Few edibles want wet feet or shade, but there are some that benefit from each (I'll let you know which). Additionally, most edibles grow best in slightly acidic soil, though some thrive in more acidic soil, while others need soil with a neutral to slightly alkaline pH. I've indicated if plants deviate from the "slightly acidic" requirements as well. *Note:* Always read seed packets and plant descriptions for specific information pertaining to each plant.

VEGETABLES

When you think of "growing food," vegetables likely come to mind first. Traditional gardening practices have always included seasonal greens and tasty tomatoes. We depend on these vegetables to enhance our meals and help our bodies absorb crucial nutrients and minerals. Growing vegetables is a time-honored hobby that provides creativity, wonder, satisfaction, and the ultimate "yard to table" experience.

The best advice I can offer is to grow what you love, *while* you love it. You may not harvest every crop that you grow, and that is okay; the moment any plant gets "ugly" pull it out, cut it down and replace it with something new. The point of a foodscape is to create an interactive, innovative and inspired space. I have a no-tolerance policy for unkempt crops, flowers, trees or shrubs.

It is important to grow the plants you enjoy eating and for which you have the appropriate climate. Some vegetables are too easy and beautiful not to grow season after season; others may not be worth the headaches of cultivating. This is a list that includes my favorite edibles that should not require excessive attention and thus are perfect for growing in common landscape spaces. Always enjoy the experience and learn from each plant. You and your foodscape will evolve over time.

ARUGULA *(Eruca vesicaria)*

Also known as rocket or roquette, small leaves of this cool season green will add spice and flavor to your fresh salads and can be served "wilted" with warm vinegar to complement hearty dishes. Arugula grows easily from seed and looks great sown in a mass along a border edge, making harvest easy and convenient. Plant in the early spring and fall.

Harvest rosettes of foliage regularly during the cool months. Similar to leaf lettuce and mustard greens, arugula will bolt (flower), stretching up in hot, sunny weather. The 15-30"-tall spikes of pale white flowers are showy and attract beneficial pollinators. Allow the plants to go to seed and self sow to create a maintenance-free groundcover. Arugula will grow during the summer, but its leaves will be much spicier.

ASPARAGUS (Asparagus officinalis)

Asparagus is one of the few commonly grown perennial edibles (living up to 20 years!). New shoots emerge in the spring and should be harvested while they are still tender. Delicious eaten raw, steamed, roasted or grilled, asparagus is a good source of vitamin B6, calcium, magnesium and zinc.

This edible originated in coastal habitats and thrives in soils that are too salty for most plants. You can grow asparagus from seed, but you'll get a quicker harvest if you plant three-year-old crowns (you can buy these at nurseries or online). Let the foliage remain once you finish harvesting. It's wispy and fernlike and serves as a perfect companion plant to tomatoes: asparagus may repel harmful root nematodes that affect tomato plants, while the tomatoes deter asparagus beetles.

BEANS (Phaseolus vulgaris)

Beans are incredibly versatile in cooking. The fresh, immature fruits are what we know as "green beans." Dry beans are the basis for soups, stews, casseroles, dips and more. Gardeners in warm regions with long growing seasons (6 months or more) can get several crops of fresh beans by sowing in succession every couple of weeks in late spring and late summer. This is a great way to extends your growing season and increase your overall harvests.

I will admit I don't grow many beans because I think harvesting can be tedious. However, bean plants are attractive in the landscape, particularly those with bright flowers like 'Scarlet Runner' or interesting pods of 'Red Swan Bush'. Bush varieties are well behaved, functioning like small shrubs. I like to plant yard-long beans (Vigna unguiculata subsp. sesquipedalis) as vines to cover walk-through tunnel entryways. The effect is interesting and it makes harvesting convenient. Also called Chinese long beans, they're definitely a talking point, too!

BOK CHOY or PAK CHOI
(Brassica rapa subsp. chinensis)

Known as Chinese cabbage, bok choy does not form a head and has smooth, dark green leaves and white stalks. This is a nutrient-dense vegetable with high levels of vitamins A, C and K. Commonly used is stir-fries and spring rolls, it can be served cooked or raw as it has a very crunchy texture and a mild flavor. Grown best in the cool season, this is an excellent candidate for mass planting with pansies or as a container specimen to add color, texture and nutrition to your favorite patio pot.

BROCCOLI (Brassica oleracea var. italica)

My favorite cool season vegetable, broccoli, is an attractive addition to common landscapes. It is easier to grow broccoli from transplants, as with all of the "head" forms of Brassicas, including cauliflower. Transplant broccoli into the garden when soil temperatures are cool in the fall and spring. If you live where soil-borne diseases are a problem, plant a "broccoli barrel" with fresh soil each spring and fall. Save yourself a lot of trouble and apply either diatomaceous earth or *Bacillus thuringiensis (Bt)* to young plants to help reduce damage caused by cutworms and cabbage moth caterpillars. Provide ample space between plants to allow the rosette of foliage to reach its full 18-24" spread. First, harvest the big main head while it is still tight. Once you harvest that, side shoot florets will form and you can harvest those, too.

The edible flower buds will open to yellow flowers if not harvested. Pollinators love those! You can collect seed from open-pollinated varieties and store it in the refrigerator for long-term viability. (See page 139 for some ornamental plant tips that can add color to your broccoli barrel.)

CABBAGE (Brassica oleracea var. capitata)

Cabbage is a plant that grows best with a pH of 6.0-6.8 and highly fertile soil. It needs a lot of nitrogen in the beginning of growth and higher amounts of phosphorous and potassium once the head has gained some size. It is a cool season vegetable that grows best in temperatures between 39-75°F. Major temperature swings can cause bolting (flowering). If temperatures are going to drop below 25°F, cover plants with a frost cloth, burlap or plastic to prevent damage. In the zone 7 central North Carolina climate I grow in, cabbage is a fall and late winter crop. In cool climates with long summer days, like Alaska, cabbages can grow to staggering sizes. I'm sure you've seen the pictures.

There are a lot of insect and disease pressures to contend with in a cabbage patch. Black rot, a bacterial disease, causes lesions starting at the leaf margins and results in wilting plants. Fungal diseases include wirestem and fusarium yellows. Root knot nematodes are a huge issue for my foodscape, which is growing on a former tobacco field. They cause stunted and wilted plants with yellow leaves. Cabbage worms are my main pest issue, and during wet winters when the Bt washes off I can lose hundreds of heads to their relentless chewing. Last spring, after not managing my Brassicaceae crops well, it appeared I had created ground-zero for this pest. Literally thousands of moths flitted about my garden. Visitors were enthralled while I was consumed with fear of having developed a mutant strain of flesh-eating cabbage worms. I will likely have

Cabbage worms

an even larger population in the future, making cabbage a more difficult crop for me to grow. When I'm not dealing with flesh-eating cabbage worms, I love to make soba noodle bowls with cabbage for extra crunch. A light dressing of rice vinegar and toasted sesame oil makes a delicious lunch.

CARROTS (*Daucus carota* subsp. *sativus*)

Carrots are easy to grow from seed and attract beneficial pollinators over a long period of time. They're host plants to the swallowtail butterfly during its caterpillar stage and they're one of the best edibles for seasonal beauty. They also have beautiful flowers that resemble those of Queen Anne's lace. If you grow an open-pollinated variety (which should be indicated on the seed packet) you can let some plants stay in the ground and flower and set seed to save.

Carrots are a cool season crop that's easy to direct sow. Layer compost 3" deep, covering the open mulch space of an existing bed. Scatter the seed on the surface of the compost, rake lightly and apply a thin (1") layer of mulch. Sow several patches of carrots in succession over a period of eight weeks to ensure a constant, fresh supply for your culinary use. Once you've tasted a carrot that you grew yourself, you'll

have a new appreciation for them. I like to roast carrots, but homegrown carrots are delicious straight out of the ground.

CAULIFLOWER
(*Brassica oleracea* var. *botrytis*)

Purple cauliflower is a fun addition to the cool season foodscape.

Cauliflower is a cool season vegetable that grows best when temperatures are below 70°F. In warm climates, grow it as a winter vegetable but cover it when temperatures drop below 15°F. The mild flavors of cauliflower make it a popular vegetable served raw or cooked in a variety of ways, including steamed, roasted and grilled.

Cauliflower comes in several different colors, with white being the most common, yet the orange varieties such as 'Cheddar' and 'Orange Bouquet' contain 25% more vitamin A than the white varieties. Green cauliflower, or Romanesco, has flower buds that form a striking fractal spiral. It's as delicious as it is pretty and has a nutty flavor. Look for 'Minaret' and 'Veronica' varieties for outstanding performance. Selections of purple-colored cauliflower like 'Graffiti' and 'Purple Cape' contain the antioxidants called anthocyanins, which are responsible for great nutrition and vibrant colors.

CELERY (Apium graveolens)

Celery may not be a staple in your everyday diet but it is a lovely plant, particularly in milder climates where it grows as a true biennial (meaning it lasts for two years). Grown from seed, its first season will produce an abundance of stalks  and foliage perfect for fresh culinary use. During the second season, the plants will develop a robust flower stalk. The flowers are insect pollinated and attract honeybees and other beneficial bugs before setting an abundant seed crop (also useful in the kitchen). Celery requires constant moisture, so plant it where you can easily water it (or in a water system) and where it is near other moisture-loving plants. Because the seeds germinate somewhat erratically, it's best to start seeds in the house or greenhouse and plant out transplants in the spring and fall.

Celery is a cooking staple and is considered part of the "holy trinity" of culinary flavoring. Along with onions and carrots, celery makes up the French mirepoix often used as a base for sauces and soups. Homegrown celery is quite a bit spicier and more flavorful than store-bought celery.

COLLARDS (Brassica oleracae var. medullosa)

Collard greens are a loose-leaf cabbage relative grown in the cool season. Very popular in the southeast U.S., collards are best picked after cold temperatures have hit. The leafy greens will regenerate through the winter, providing ample harvests for a long period of time. Germination occurs in under 10 days; seeds can be sown directly in place as a ground cover. The plants are tough, withstanding harsh conditions, including cold and drought.

CORN (Zea mays)

The most abundantly-grown crop in the world, corn was domesticated about 10,000 years ago. It may seem like an unusual plant to include in your home landscape, but the bold texture and overall size of the plants make corn a dynamic addition. Sow corn directly in a full sun border in clumps for a more traditional, organized style. Use corn as an exclamation point in the garden or as a seasonal edible property border. Corn in the landscape is definitely a conversation piece, I can tell you that!

Choose varieties from the six major types depending on your culinary needs: dent corn, flint corn, pod corn, popcorn, flour corn and sweet corn. I like to grow heirloom varieties, Bloody Butcher in particular, which I grind into grits and eat throughout the year. For traditional fresh culinary use, select varieties of sweet corn like 'Silver Queen'. It is easy and delicious grilled. Simply pull the husk leaves down and remove the silks. Fold the leaves back up so they cover the kernels and soak the ears in water for 10 minutes. Place the corn ears on the grill for 20 minutes with the lid closed, rotating every five minutes. Remove from grill and roll in butter, squeeze a bit of lime juice on the corn ears and sprinkle with smoked paprika.

Dried heirloom corn varieties including 'Bloody Butcher' (bottom right red) and 'Dwarf Popcorn' (middle) are a colorful addition to the Thanksgiving table.

CUCUMBER *(Cucumis sativus)*

Cucumbers are a summer staple for most gardeners. They have either a creeping, vine habit (plants grow best when trained off of the ground) or a bush habit that will grow well in a bed or border without support. Full sun and frequent, even watering are critical to having high yields of consistent quality. The fruits develop quickly, so check plants daily during harvest season.

There are three main varieties of cucumber: slicing, pickling and burpless. The cylindrical fruits are abundant and can be eaten sliced fresh or made into delicious cold summer soups. My favorite reason to grow cukes is to make "refrigerator dill pickles."

Common pests include the potato beetle, flea beetle, aphids and spider mites, which can be controlled by applying *Bacillus thuringiensis (Bt)*, a bacterium that attacks the soft-bodied larvae.

Eggplant is an important edible in Asian and Indian cuisine. It becomes tender when cooked, developing a rich, complex flavor. I slice eggplants into cubes and soak them in a salt water bath for five minutes to reduce bitterness and draw out some of the water. Then I lightly toss with olive or grape seed oil and add seasonings for roasting, sautéing and grilling. They are yummy when stuffed and grilled. The skins develop a unique charred appearance and flavor.

EGGPLANT *(Solanum melongena)*

This is the vegetable with an identity crisis. Ever wonder what "eggplant" actually means? It is a common name (as opposed to the botanical name *Solanum melongena*) describing the white or yellow fruits of 18th century European cultivars that resembled goose eggs.

Best grown from seed started in pots inside a warm greenhouse, eggplants thrive in full sun with moist, rich soil through the heat of the summer.

FENNEL *(Foeniculum vulgare)*

This hardy perennial herb is native to the Mediterranean region and will tolerate dry soils and low fertility. Used as the primary ingredient in Absinthe, the anise flavor is an acquired taste. My favorite variety for culinary use is the Florence fennel, a selection with a swollen, bulb-like stem that can be sliced thinly and served raw over salad greens. It is also delicious roasted with a sprinkle of salt and olive oil. Well suited for full sun, fennel is an important source of food for the swallowtail caterpillar.

GARLIC *(Allium sativum)*

This is one of my all-time favorite edibles to grow! Garlic belongs along the edge of every landscape. I have come to the conclusion that nearly every person has the ability to grow all of the garlic they consume in a year. It is easy to grow with very little maintenance and can be contained to the edge along any sunny border during the cool season.

A simple method for growing garlic is via vegetative division: simply thumb in the raw individual cloves along the fronts of the garden beds. Every clove will develop into a bulb over the season, providing ample access to homegrown, organic garlic. Buying organic garlic is actually a great way to give growing a try. *Bonus:* garlic plants help to deter in-ground pests such as voles.

Plant garlic along bed edges for ease of planting and harvest. This typically unused space can add up to a year's worth of garlic and helps deter in ground mammals like Voles!

Write on a painted brick with weatherproof marker to keep track of your variety names and planting dates.

Make easy garlic bread by slicing a loaf of crusty bread into ¾" pieces and toasting lightly. Then rub a peeled clove of raw garlic over the bread, top with a thin slice of parmesan cheese and broil until the cheese is bubbly. My kitchen rule is: "Do not sit down while the broiler is on!" (You'll regret it if you do – trust me.)

KALE (*Brassica oleracea* var. *sabellica*)

This super food has reinvigorated the widespread use of greens and happens to be one of the most attractive and easy-to-grow landscape plants. Grow kale from seed sown either directly in the ground or in  seed flats for spring and fall transplanting. This cool season crop prefers soil temperatures between 40°F and 70°F. As temperatures rise, a tall stalk of attractive yellow flowers will bolt from the center of the plant, providing pollen and nectar for beneficial insects before setting seed, which you can collect and sow during the next cool season.

Like all of the Brassica crops, young kale plants are a magnet for cabbage and cut worms. Dust the kale with *Bt* regularly to avoid severe damage and crop loss. Kale also makes an excellent "edible mulch" to shade the soil and out-compete weeds when sown in a mass and is also a tidy border plant. It grows well mixed with flowering plants such as pansies, violas and snapdragons during the spring, fall and winter (depending on where you live). Pick young kale leaves and throw them in salad. The best way to eat "grown up" kale is to remove the midribs, shred it into small strips (think paper-shredder-sized strips) and massage with a little bit of salt and lemon juice or flavored vinegar.

LETTUCE (*Lactuca sativa*)

With hundreds of cultivars to choose from, lettuce can provide dynamic color and texture in the cool season garden. The leaf lettuce selections are best sown in a mass directly along edges or in containers for easy harvest. As the plants develop, harvest by trimming the top half of the leaves. This will allow the plants to continue growing for a long season. Heading forms can be started in pots and transplanted into the garden to ensure proper spacing. You can harvest the whole plant as needed when heads are approximately 8-12" wide.

Lettuce is famous for turning bitter when the flowers bolt from warm days. Let Mother Nature do all the work for you by allowing some plants to set seed and self sow.

Oakleaf and Curly Red Leaf lettuce make a beautiful contrast in the landscape.

MALABAR SPINACH (*Basella alba* 'Rubra')

This "vine spinach" is a fast-growing, herbaceous vine ideal for climates with hot summers. The heart-shaped leaves have a mild flavor and are high in vitamins A and C, iron and calcium. It makes an excellent substitution for

lettuce in the summer. I grow it along porch rails for easy harvest.

There are two varieties available – green and red. The stem of the *Basella alba* is green and the stem of the cultivar *Basella alba*, or 'Rubra', is reddish-purple; both have solid green foliage and shiny purple/black berries that can easily reseed the following season. Add the leaves to summer salads and smoothies.

MIZUNA (*Brassica rapa*)

Mizuna is a Japanese green with a peppery flavor excellent for stir-fries or eaten raw as salad. The finely dissected foliage is attractive and colorful, as there are many varieties to grow from seed. Like most greens, mizuna performs best in mild climates with temperatures under 85°F. I grow it as a cool season crop seeding it in August and February and harvesting for 6 months each year.

ONIONS (*Allium cepa*)

Onions are an exceptionally attractive, low-maintenance crop to include in your foodscape, especially because they're a staple in the kitchen. Similar to garlic, onions are easily grown from vegetative division and are often sold as "sets" or small bulbs. They prefer to grow in well-drained, cool soil and need to be planted close to the surface to develop a large bulb. Cut the flower spikes to the ground when they appear in order to allow the energy to go into bulb production rather than seed. The foliage will yellow to brown when the plants are mature, alerting you that it is time to harvest.

Onions are a great edge-to-mid-border plant and are effective for deterring in-ground mammals such as moles and voles. I find homegrown, organic onions to be stronger compared to the watery store-bought selections and they last for a long time in cold, dark storage, similar to a potato. They can also be sliced, blanched and frozen for long-term storage.

PARSNIP *(Pastinaca sativa)*

Closely related to the carrot, parsnip is a biennial root vegetable grown as a cool season annual. Cultivated for its long, cream-colored tuberous root, it is best grown through the winter, as it becomes sweeter in flavor after hard frosts. A good source of potassium, parsnips can be eaten raw or cooked and are traditionally used in winter stews and pot pies. Sow parsnip in full sun and loose, fertile soil for success.

PEANUTS *(Arachis hypogaea)*

This is my favorite summer edging plant. Peanuts are too easy to grow not to try at least once. Plants develop into 24" masses with yellow flowers that are attractive all summer. Their drought tolerance makes peanuts practical even in landscapes with no irrigation. As legumes, they naturally fix nitrogen in the soil, providing nutrients for the plants surrounding them.

Peanuts are easy to grow from a raw (unroasted) nut. When the soil temperature is consistently warm (above 65°F), thumb single (shelled) nuts into the ground 1-2" deep and about 8" apart. They will germinate in 6-10 days and grow through the warm season. They are a crop that does best in hot climates with long growing seasons. I have heard accounts, however, of people successfully growing them into zone 5. As the temperatures get cool and the days grow shorter, the foliage will begin to turn yellow signifying harvest time. This is a fun and easy process as you literally yank the plants out of the ground and find the nuts growing on the roots.

An average plant can have 12-25 nuts, making a foundation landscape edge an abundant resource for homegrown, organic peanuts. Harvest when you have a dry forecast, as they will need a few days to "cure" in the sun once removed from the soil. Turn the plants "nut side up" in place or on a tarp to allow them to dry in the autumn sunshine.

Once the nuts have dried in the sun, you can cook them and begin eating. Raw peanuts, when consumed in mass, can cause stomach aches, so I recommend only eating cooked peanuts. And since I am not a native Southerner I do not indulge in boiled peanuts. However, many people claim they are a delicacy. Instead, I roast my crop and have discovered that shelled peanuts cook more quickly and consistently. Place the shelled peanuts on a baking sheet in a 400°F oven for 45 minutes, checking every 15 minutes and shaking the pan to move the nuts around. You can add salt before or after. Sample the nuts for your desired crunchiness and allow to cool before serving. They are bound to be a big hit with kids and adults and make an excellent gift for friends and family.

PEPPERS (Capsisum spp.)

Peppers are all the rage these days, especially with hipster millennials who like to test their limits for heat tolerance. I prefer to grow easy-to-eat bell peppers, including jalapeños, Serrano and Marconi. A good rule of thumb with peppers is the hotter they are, the more abundant the harvest. Then you have to figure out what to do with all those too-hot-to-eat peppers. One habanero plant is more than enough for a year of consumption, whereas you may need 20 bell pepper plants to produce enough for half the year.

Peppers are slow to germinate from seed, so start them indoors and wait to plant until well after night temperatures are consistently above 50°F. Peppers love heat and will fruit abundantly as the days become shorter. Requiring much less water and fertility compared to other summer crops, peppers are practical to grow throughout borders, in containers, and will even produce fruit in partial shade.

Candied peppers are one of my favorite culinary indulgences. It is a great way to preserve them and serve with nearly any meal. Find the recipe on page 169. Peppers can also be sliced, blanched and frozen, pickled, or roasted and processed into a soup base.

POTATOES (Solanum tuberosum)

Every kid loves French fries, so why not teach them where their favorite food comes from? Potatoes are a low-maintenance crop that can produce an abundance of edible tubers through the spring and fall. I grow my 'taters the old-fashioned way – in the ground. As old potatoes begin to sprout inside the house, I cut the growing eyes off in chunks and allow the pieces to dry for several days inside. Then, I plant those vegetative "cuttings" along the edges of my borders by digging a 15-18" trench and dropping a piece every 8". Cover the trench, add some slow release fertilizer, water in and walk away; 3-4 months later it will be time to harvest. The foliage will turn yellow, signaling that it is time to dig.

Always use a wide-tined fork to harvest potatoes. This will reduce the number of tubers that get stabbed (which causes rapid decay). Post-harvest, I store the unwashed potatoes in brown bags inside my pantry (and bedroom closets) for several weeks before starting to cook them. This allows the sugars to settle into starch.

You can easily grow more than 100 pounds of potatoes along a foundation landscape edge. I leave the smallest tubers in the ground, ensuring the next season's harvest and am never without homegrown, organically-raised potatoes.

SHALLOTS *(Allium cepa var. aggregatum)*

Shallots are a type of onion that grows in clusters, similar to garlic. Plant them near the surface of the ground, keeping the top of the bulb above ground. In northern regions of the U.S. and into Canada, shallots can be planted in late winter when the ground has frozen – they will mature by the end of summer. Shallots are delicious sliced thin and served raw, sautéed and added to soups, or deep fried – as they are commonly served in Asia. Like their Allium relatives, shallots are a low-maintenance crop that can be planted along bed edges for easy harvest.

SNAP PEAS *(Pisum sativum var. macrocarpon)*

Like all other peas, sugar snap peas are pod fruits containing 3-8 peas per pod. Similar to a garden or English pea, snaps have a less-fibrous pod and are edible when young. The pods differ from snow peas in that they are round, not flat, and do not open when they are ripe.

Pea plants are climbing and require sturdy staking or a trellis for optimal growth. Some cultivars can grow more than 6' in a season! I don't always grow snap peas because I find the harvest to be tedious, and they can take up a considerable amount of real estate. However, snap peas are a delicacy that every person should grow at least once in their lifetime and can make a bold statement in the landscape. They are delicious eaten right from the vine when the flowers at the ends of the pods have just withered. There are varieties with edible pods which are delicious in stir-fries.

SOYBEANS (Glycine max)

Soy is a species of legume native to East Asia and is widely grown for its edible bean that has numerous uses. It is easy to grow across the U.S. and Canada as a warm season crop that is attractive and fixes nitrogen. In fact, the U.S. cultivates more than 30% of the annual soy crops distributed globally. Soy is a wonderful little legume and can supply abundant and delicious additions to your culinary ventures. I keep it easy with my soybean crops because edamame (harvested while the soy beans are still young) is one of my favorite snacks! I harvest the pods green and tender and steam them with a light dusting of salt and cumin.

Rabbits can be a major pest. One year, bunnies ate more than 300 young plants in my front border. I now grow my soybeans in amongst peppers instead of as an edge plant where they can too-easily be browsed. If rabbits are not a problem where you live, soybeans make great edging plants.

SWEET POTATOES (Ipomoea batatas)

Sweet potatoes are only distantly related to the common potato and are not part of the nightshade family. Commonly grown for their ornamental foliage attributes, they produce large, starchy, sweet-tasting, tuberous roots that can be stored for long periods of time. The vines can grow 8-15' long and make a beautiful groundcover. Harvest by digging with a potato fork and allowing the tubers to dry on the soil surface. Frequently used as a side at Thanksgiving, sweet potatoes are a delicious addition to any meal.

RADISH (Raphanus sativus)

Radishes are cool season root vegetables varying in size, flavor, color and length of time they take to mature. They owe the sharp flavor of their roots to the various chemical compounds produced by the plant and are often grown as companion plants because they suffer from few pests and diseases. Seeds germinate quickly and grow rapidly, with small varieties being ready for consumption within a month. Larger daikon varieties can take up to 90 days to mature. Radishes are also useful when planted as a cover crop in the cool season. You can till the foliage into the soil to deter root knot nematodes.

Both roots and leaves can be served cooked or raw. But I think radishes taste best when eaten fresh from the garden. Thinly grate them and add them raw to your favorite salads. They are great for pickling, too.

SPINACH (Spinacia oleracea)

A rich source of vitamin A, spinach is a cool season green that is delicious and beautiful. Easily grown from seed sown directly into the landscape, spinach is a long season crop in climates with mild summers. In areas with more extreme temperatures, sow spinach in a weekly succession to extend the harvest. Spinach will bolt when days get long and temperatures soar. Add spinach to frittatas, smoothies, salads, lasagnas — anything! It's also delicious when sautéed with a little garlic and olive oil.

SQUASH: SUMMER *(Cucurbita pepo)*

This includes cousa squash, pattypan (scallop squash), tromboncino or zucchetta, crookneck, straightneck and zucchini (courgette). Summer squash, though easy to grow, can be cumbersome when dealing with the abundant harvest – the classic feast-or-famine crop. It is best sown directly in place. Thumb the seed into moist compost that is 1" deep. Plant in areas with full sun that have easy access to water, as squash will under-perform in dry conditions. This is definitely a foodscape Zone 1 plant – close to the house! Seeds take about a week to germinate and the long, ground-covering vines will sprawl across the ground reaching up to 6' long. Once pollination has occurred and fruits begin to develop, daily harvests will be necessary.

Squash bugs are often the culprit for sudden death of squash. There are organic pest controls available, but I simply remove infested plants and continue to sow seed on a bi-weekly rotation from April to July to ensure a succession of harvest.

SQUASH: WINTER *(Curcubita* spp.)

This includes hard shell squash like butternut, pumpkins and gourds.

Similar to soft shell squash, these varieties are easily grown from seed directly sown into the landscape. Plant winter squash vines in areas with ample space, sunlight and water. These vines will attach to structures, fences and other plants with long tendrils, making them suitable for use as a screen feature. It takes 3-4 months to grow a winter squash plant to maturity.

Most often, the foliage will senesce, turning crisp and brown, before the fruit is ready to be harvested. Considering the sprawling habit of winter squash, it may not be the best choice, from an aesthetic perspective, for a foundation landscape; however, having homegrown pumpkins to carve for Halloween is an experience that everyone deserves to enjoy. Butternut squash is also a fabulous autumnal addition to soups and casseroles.

TOMATILLOS (Physalis philadelphica)

Originally from Mexico, the "husk tomato" is an easy-to-grow, low-maintenance, drought-tolerant alternative to traditional tomatoes. They grow quite large through the heat of the summer and begin to set fruit as the days grow shorter. The green fruits are round, and, as the common name indicates, have a papery husk protecting the fruit. Harvest when the husk begins to break open due to the swollen fruit. Used as a primary ingredient in salsa verde, tomatillos can be eaten raw or boiled for a short period time to soften the flesh for culinary use.

TOMATOES (Solanum lycopersicum)

Tomatoes, my favorite crop of the summer season, are full of challenges. From soil-borne disease to insect pressure, getting the ultimate taste of summer can require some serious devotion, especially in hot and humid climates like the one I garden in. However, the effort is always worthwhile when, on a cold January night, you enjoy a bowl of heirloom tomato soup – from tomatoes grown in your garden – while browsing seed catalogs. It's amazing how the lingering memories of hard work, extra watering and constant trimming can fade away when you take that first spoonful of mouth-watering deliciousness.

Heirloom tomatoes are my "thing" and I have become quite snobby about the flavorless hybrids that are so commonly sold in grocery stores. Of course, the heirlooms have been selected for taste and color, not disease resistance, so if you want

to grow heirlooms, be prepared to try several cultivars to see which perform best in your climate.

There are many definitions of what makes an heirloom an heirloom. My general thought is that it should be an open-pollinated variety that has been in circulation for more than 60 years, meaning it pre-dates the 1940s. Classic selections such as 'Mortgage Lifter' come with fun historic tales of times long past (can you imagine paying your mortgage off from selling tomatoes?) with a delicious fruit. They deservedly have a cult following. I say, "Once you go heirloom you never go back." And then you will have to grow a ton because you will never buy another grocery store tomato again.

Tomatoes are grown from seed started indoors with warm soil temperatures. Use a seedling heat mat under the trays to speed up the germination time. Be sure to only sow one seed per pot, or thin to one seedling upon germinating. Plants that are crowded will under-perform because of competition for resources. Similar to peppers, tomatoes will not grow in cool, wet soil. Wait to transplant into the garden until night temperatures are over 50°F.

You need to consider size when choosing tomato varieties. Most heirlooms are indeterminate, meaning they continue growing all season and set flowers and fruit for many months on the same growth. This is great for growers in warm climates to extend the harvest season; but when your indeterminate tomatoes have vines growing upwards of 20' long, they will require serious staking. Over the past decade I have tried many different stakes and have finally settled on 10-15' sections of cattle fencing. This sturdy wire holds the vines upright and can be used season after season. I also like to plant big, unruly tomatoes on the southeast side of large deciduous flowering shrubs, such as 'Limelight' hydrangea. These living stakes provide the structural integrity for the tomato vines to climb through and hide the sometimes unattractive foliage.

Many of the best paste varieties are semi-determinate, meaning they grow to a more manageable-sized vine of up to 10' long with a multi-branch habit. You can use a traditional tiered cage to contain these and add a central stake that you can tie the tips to in order to help with air flow and access for harvest. My favorite tomato, 'Cream Sausage', fits into this category and makes a handsome plant that is size-appropriate for even formal landscapes.

The modern "bush" hybrids do offer an attractive size for containers, but they generally lack the dynamic flavor that I have grown accustomed to.

I started growing tomatoes hydroponically as a patio feature. It is always a conversation-starter and the yields far exceed that of the in-ground tomatoes. (See page 145 for hydroponics information.) Here in central North Carolina it is hard to find a piece of land that wasn't under tobacco cultivation at some point in history, and the soil-borne diseases and root knot nematodes make it challenging to grow tomatoes in the ground.

One way to reduce this issue is to graft your desired heirloom cultivar onto a disease-resistant rootstock. This isn't foolproof but will increase the yields and growing season compared to plants on their own roots. Grafted heirlooms are starting to become more popular and can be found via mail order and in some independent garden centers.

Tomatoes are the most popular edible in the American diet. All gardeners and foodscapers should at least try to grow a few of their own, if for no other reason but to develop a greater respect for the availability that commercial agriculture has created. I have several recipes for processing and using tomatoes. Look for those starting on page 164.

to beneficial pollinators and can provide ample seed for seasons to come if allowed to ripen.

One of my favorite moments in my Foodscape Revolution occurred in December in my edible entry turnip patch. The neighborhood children were helping me harvest for the holiday party I was hosting. They had never seen or tasted turnips before and were skeptical, to say the least. I scrubbed the skins clean, cubed the white, fleshy roots and tossed them into bread pans with some salt, garlic and butter and then into a 400°F oven. Fast forward 45 minutes and the turnip roots had caramelized and were the hit of the party.

TURNIPS (*Brassica rapa* subsp. *Rapa*)

I think turnips are the most under-appreciated of the root vegetables and I'm waiting for them to have a massive comeback. The ease of growing and cold hardiness, plus the mild, buttery flavor of the roots, make this a must-grow in the foodscape. They're packed with nutrients and have a long growing season.

Seed will germinate quickly when sown directly in the sunny landscape on well-drained compost. This cool season vegetable prefers air temperatures below 70°F and will bolt as temperatures increase. The flowers are attractive

Harvesting turnips from the neighborhood entrance planting

HERBS

Adding fresh flavor to home cooking is one of the simplest pleasures of growing plants. Herbs are hardy and easy to incorporate into the everyday landscape. Many are evergreen and perennial with low water and fertility needs. Used fresh or dried homegrown, herbs add a special touch of authenticity to every meal.

This list represents the herbs that I have come to love and adore both for aesthetic value in the foodscape and for practical culinary use.

BASIL *(Ocimum basilicum)*

One of the most recognizable and commonly grown herbs, basil is a summer staple in the foodscape. The glossy green foliage can be eaten raw or dried for long-term culinary use. Traditional kitchen basil will grow into a mounded specimen up to 3' tall and wide. The white flowers produced on the tip of each branch should be removed to maintain the mild flavor of the leaves.

There are many varieties available, with variegated or purple foliage and dwarf habits to meet the diverse needs of every garden and container. The small leaf forms are excellent grown along a bed edge, providing a boxwood-like formal appearance. Fresh-flavored lemon and lime basil can be used to spice up anything from salad to cocktails.

Small leaf basil varieties stay compact and can be grown as a hedge.

Long-term preservation is easy: use a food processor to convert large batches of fresh foliage into basil paste. Add a touch of olive oil and a pinch of salt. Fill quart-sized freezer bags and store in freezer for future use as pesto and soup and sauce flavoring.

Cilantro flowers have a lacy texture and attract pollinators.

CILANTRO/CORIANDER (Coriandrum sativum)

Most people do not realize that the fresh foliage of cilantro and the dried seed of coriander are the product of the same plant. The foliage referred to as cilantro is a staple in Latin dishes and grows with great vigor through the cool season. This plant is a short-lived annual; the flower stalks will emerge when warm temperatures and long days arrive. The showy white flowers attract pollinators and beneficial insects. Allow the flowers to go to seed and fully dry before harvesting the seed. Do not try to grow during the middle of summer; you'll be disappointed (it's not you, it's the plant).

The foliage (cilantro leaves) can be harvested throughout the short life cycle and can be preserved for up to three weeks in the refrigerator. It can also be saved by food processing the raw greens and then freezing them in one-quart bags. You can then add the greens to soups, stir-fries, salsa and more throughout the remainder of the year.

DILL (Anethum graveolens)

I may be a bit biased here, but I think every gardener should be growing dill! It is simply too easy to grow and too beautiful not to be sown in a mass. Dill performs great through the hot summers, but foliage must be harvested early in the growing cycle as dill is a major food source for swallowtail butterfly caterpillars, who can easily consume entire plants in a matter of days.

Dill is best grown from seed directly sown on the surface of rich organic matter. It can reach 36" tall when in full flower and looks dynamic against conifer textures in the landscape. Snip leaves for use in salads, and harvest seed by cutting the flower heads off of the stalks as the seed begins to ripen (turn tan in color). Place the seed heads upside-down in a paper bag or bucket for ease of collecting. Seeds can be dry stored for culinary use or kept in cool, dry storage for sowing the next season.

Swallowtail caterpillars will devour dill in a matter of days

LAVENDER (*Lavandula* spp.)

Lavender is an Old World Mediterranean native that thrives in that typical hot, dry climate, which means it's difficult to grow in humid locations. You must have well-drained soil in order to grow lavender. If your foodscape is soggy, plant lavender in a pot. New varieties with strong performance and vigor such as 'Phenomenal' and 'Platinum Blonde', however, are making lavender a viable landscape option in more locations. In cooler areas, wait until plants have started to leaf out in the spring to cut back growth that might have been killed during the winter.

Lavender's purple flower spikes attract honeybees and other beneficial pollinators while providing the tantalizing scent known for relaxation. Flowers are used to scent household products, but they can also be used to bake cookies, make lemonade and infuse cocktails. Experiment! Let me warn you, though, a little bit of lavender goes a long way.

OREGANO (*Origanum vulgare*)

Grown as an annual in colder climates, oregano is a delicious groundcover for sunny landscapes and is perennial in warmer areas. The purple flowers and olive-green leaves are attractive and edible. Oregano prefers hot, relatively dry climates, but adapts well in moist, well-drained garden soils. It can become almost weedy when it's happy!

In general, the cold-hardy varieties of oregano have a milder flavor. 'Aurea' is my favorite variety to grow; the bright yellow foliage is attractive, and the flavor is the perfect addition to my homegrown tomato sauce (recipe on page 168).

PARSLEY *(Petroselinum crispum)*

Parsley is easy to grow from transplants but hard to grow from seed. I usually buy a tray of 48 plants and plant them throughout my foodscape. I think it's impossible to overplant parsley. Grow in the cool

season (spring and fall – and through the winter in the warmest areas). Parsley pairs well with alyssum, violas and other cool season flowers. Parsley also is a nice, edible addition to winter container gardens.

The main reason I grow parsley in my foodscape every year is that it attracts several species of wildlife. It is favored by swallowtail butterflies as a host plant for their larvae; their caterpillars are black and green striped with yellow dots and will feed on parsley for two weeks before turning into butterflies. Bees and other nectar-feeding insects also visit the flowers, and goldfinches will feed on the seeds.

If you have an abundance of parsley, you'll find yourself adding it to salads, soups, sandwiches – basically everything. It adds such a fresh flavor and burst of nutrients. Parsley: it's not just a garnish.

ROSEMARY *(Rosmarinus officinalis)*

Rosemary is another Mediterranean-region native. It is a woody perennial with needle-like evergreen leaves. Because it is attractive and drought tolerant, rosemary is commonly used as an ornamental plant across the world. Growing it in full sun, in soil with good drainage and a neutral-to-slightly-alkaline pH (7-7.8), will ensure long-term success.

Rosemary is sensitive to "wet feet" and does not tolerate extreme cold or a heavy snow load. Here in central North Carolina, where we endure cold and wet through the winter season, rosemary will

frequently defoliate and have branch dieback from sudden cold snaps. 'Arp' and 'Salem' are two reliable varieties with good flavor and an

upright, vigorous habit. While rosemary is popular for training as a hedge or topiary, I prefer the groundcover or trailing cultivars such as 'Prostratus' for container cultivation because they spread widely with a dense and durable texture.

Rosemary is a staple in many classic dishes. I love to add it to potato dishes and always throw a fresh branch into the slow cooker when making a pot roast.

THYME *(Thymus vulgaris)*

This evergreen herb is easy to grow and has culinary, medicinal and ornamental value. The small foliage grows as a thick groundcover that tolerates light foot traffic. It performs best in full sun with well-drained soil, and is useful to grow along steep banks to help control erosion. There are many selections available including fuzzy foliage, gold leaves and variegation to increase landscape appeal. Thyme, fresh or dried, is a delicious addition to any meal. It is also delicious in lemonade!

SAGE *(Salvia officinalis)*

Sage has been used since ancient times for warding off evil, healing snakebites and increasing women's fertility. By the Middle Ages, sage had developed both a medicinal reputation and culinary use, which has continued.

Sage is a small flowering shrub grown best in full sun with well-drained soil. It is treated as an herbaceous annual in many climates, and is a great addition to container planting, rock gardens and foundation landscapes. Considered an "essential herb," its dried foliage has a savory, slightly peppery flavor and is a staple for many beef and chicken dishes.

Five

WHAT TO PLANT:
Fruits, Nuts, Berries & Grains

AS I MENTIONED in the previous chapter, the edible plants I'll be describing need to be planted in full sun in medium-moist, well-drained soil. There are a few exceptions, though, and I will let you know about those as we go along. Also, while most of the edible plants like a "slightly acidic" soil pH, there are some that don't, and I'll note those as well. As always when you plant seeds, be sure to read the information on the seed packet.

FRUITS

This is the "less maintenance short list" of fruits because sometimes growing fruit can be a challenge. In tropical climates, a wide range of fruits, including citrus, can be easily grown, but for the majority of us living in the temperate climates of USDA zones 3-8, our options are more limited. Stone fruits such as apples, apricots, peaches and pears can suffer from late spring freezes and diverse insect and disease problems. Because I am an organic grower in the humid climate of central North Carolina, I stick to the fruits that I can grow without applying harsh chemicals or fear of crop loss due to our fickle spring temperature swings. I also like to grow native fruits that are easy-care and difficult to find in the supermarket.

BLUEBERRIES (*Vaccinium* spp.)

Native to North America, blueberries are the ideal starter plants for foodscape design. They add tons of aesthetic beauty to every landscape. White flowers in spring attract beneficial pollinators, followed by the delicious fruits of the summer, while the brilliant red fall color is a feature in and of itself. The exfoliating bark on the multi-stem branches adds winter interest.

Blueberries can be used in many ways in the home landscape: as single specimens throughout a border or as a seasonal screen, hedge, or foundation plant. Prune new growth throughout the growing season to reach the desired height and choose varieties based on the suitability of their ultimate size to their location. Many new cultivars have been bred for dwarf growing habits, making them ideal for small gardens and patio containers.

Often, you will be told to plant more than one variety because blueberries are not self-fertile and need a different variety nearby for pollination and fruit set. It is important when selecting varieties that you choose more than one cultivar that blooms at the same time, such as 'Sunshine Blue' and 'Powder Blue' together, to ensure cross-pollination, which will result in the formation of fruit.

There are many selections available in the market today. I recommend varieties that will cover a long fruiting season to extend your harvest. Most will flower at the same time and the bees will do all the pollinating for you.

Blueberry bushes are acid-loving plants, similar to azaleas, rhododendrons and camellias. Amend the soil surrounding the hole with ground pine bark. This will ensure a lower pH level, allowing the plants to absorb micronutrients more efficiently. Apply an acid-based organic fertilizer once a year for best growth and development.

During one unseasonably warm December, I noticed an early flowering tendency in some of my shrubs. The warmer temperatures resulted in one cultivar blooming out entirely. Of course it did not get cross-pollinated and when winter did finally arrive, in mid-January, all of the flower buds were frozen off. As our climate changes, we will have to be prepared for more unusual situations like this one.

BLACKBERRIES *(Rubus spp.)*

Historically, blackberries were the bramble that ate your landscape, a garden never to be found again. Between the thorns, the spreading habit and the Japanese beetles these plants can attract, blackberries have been out of favor (and out of cultivation) by home gardeners for decades. However, modern advancements in breeding have resulted in new varieties that are much better specimens for small spaces.

Now blackberries will fruit on new wood, allowing you to effectively "mow over" or cut the patch to the ground every fall. This cultural practice will help eliminate weeds (aka tree seedlings) from establishing and reduces the bloodshed overall. Because they are so drought tolerant, blackberries are a great addition to property borders and island beds where irrigation access can be limited. Blackberries freeze well and 4 or 5 plants will give you plenty of fruit for all of your baking and smoothie-making needs.

PAW PAW (*Asimina triloba*)

When I moved to North Carolina I had never heard of paw paws. In fact, I thought people were referencing their grandfathers when talking about these trees and was very confused while hiking through the Carolina hardwood forest when my guide pointed up to the "paw paw tree." As a grower of trees and shrubs, I quickly became obsessed with this native edible, mostly because the spring flowers are strange and the fact that the tasty fruit that follows is pretty awesome.

Paw paws grow across eastern North America stretching from USDA zones 3-8. They form colonies from root suckers that often represent only one genotype – which eliminates the plant's ability to access cross-pollination and fruit set. In the landscape, it is recommended that you grow more than one variety and site the trees near one another to ensure pollination occurs.

Similar to persimmon, when the fruit ripens you will be competing with night-active mammals like raccoons and possums for your harvest. I recommend harvesting and storing the fruit in the freezer, which will give it the consistency of custard. The flavor is delicious; paw paws taste like a strawberry and a banana mixed together.

PERSIMMON (*Diospyros* spp., hybrids and cultivars)

I was first introduced to persimmons while attending college in Indiana. A friend handed me a (very) unripe fruit and proceeded to fall to the ground laughing as I was left with more than a bitter mouthful of cotton after taking a bite. It took me a few years to warm up to the idea of eating persimmon again, but I am glad I did. The ripe fruit of persimmon is a life-changing delicacy, one that you will only experience from wild foraging or home cultivation as the fruits do not transport well, making them hard to find in grocery stores.

Persimmon trees are native to several parts of the world, including eastern North America and Asia. I prefer the inter-specific hybrids of these two species, which boast large fruits that ripen before frost. Grow in full sun and average soil conditions. The fall color is matched only by the graceful form and fruit set, which look like small pumpkins dangling from the ends of branches. These are large trees, though, so plan accordingly when deciding where to site them.

Highly coveted by every mammal, the fruits can be harvested before they are fully ripe (which is indicated by softness to the touch) and stored in brown bags to speed the ripening process and beat the critters. They are delicious raw or used in baking and making ice cream. One of my favorite ways to eat persimmons is the world-famous Indiana persimmon pudding, which changed my opinion about these fruits forever.

RASPBERRIES (*Rubus idaeus*)

Raspberries can be cultivated in USDA hardiness zones 3-9 and have traditionally been planted as dormant canes in fall. Recent breakthroughs in breeding have created the new market of potted, ready-to-fruit plants that are ideal for almost every landscape.

In addition to the delicious sweet fruit, the flowers are a major nectar source for honeybees and other pollinators. The vigorous growing habit can be locally invasive if not managed seasonally. The plants propagate from basal shoots, also known as suckers, and new canes can appear some distance from the original plant. For this reason, raspberries are best planted in landscapes with poorer/drier soils to help reduce the invasive growing habit. Raspberry freezer jam is just about one of the most delicious ice cream toppings you can make.

STRAWBERRIES (*Fragaria ananassa*)

Perhaps the easiest of the traditional fruits to grow and include in the landscape, strawberries are an ideal evergreen groundcover (in mild climates). Many new varieties are day-neutral, meaning they flower and set fruit even through the long days of the summer, and have bright pink or white flowers to add color and interest to the landscape. The spreading or stoloniferous habit also makes strawberries ideal specimens for hanging baskets. After harvesting your own strawberries from along the front walkway, you will discover the beauty, inspiration and purpose behind the Foodscape Revolution. Of course, strawberries are delicious for desserts, but I love to throw them in a spinach salad with candied pecans, blue cheese, finely chopped red onions and balsamic vinaigrette dressing.

WATERMELON (*Citrullus lanatus*)

A large, sprawling vine native to Africa, watermelon is actually a special kind of berry with a hard rind. A traditional summer fare, the sweet, juicy flesh is refreshing on a hot day. Many varieties are available to grow from seed and considerable efforts have been made in developing disease-resistant strains that can be grafted onto for enhanced performance. Grow in full sun and supply adequate moisture; as the name implies, this "melon" is mostly water!

NUTS

Nut trees offer the benefits of shade, fall color, wildlife habitat and delicious snacks that have a long shelf life. Though many nut trees grow best in tropical climates, there are a few highly desirable options for the average North American garden.

ALMONDS *(Prunus dulcis)*

Almonds are best grown in Mediterranean climates with warm, dry summers and mild, wet winters. The optimal temperature for growing almonds to harvest is between 59-86°F. They also need to have experienced 300-600 hours of temperatures below 45°F. If your climate zone meets that requirement, an almond can be a great ornamental tree with edible attributes. The pink flowers are bee-pollinated, which has resulted in the largest annual managed pollination where almonds are grown commercially – California – with close to one million hives being trucked into the orchards. That is nearly half the beehives in all of the United States.

Almonds are nutritionally-dense foods that can be ground into gluten-free alternatives to wheat flour for use in cooking and baking.

Fresh Hazelnuts ready to be cracked and roasted

HAZELNUTS *(Corylus americana, C. avellena and the interspecific hybrids of hope)*

The most suitable nut tree for residential settings, hazelnuts are on the brink of mass re-introduction. Thanks to the breeding efforts of Dr. Thomas Molnar of Rutgers University, new disease-resistant varieties will soon be available for East Coast growers.

Not only do hazelnuts offer a delicious and abundant nut set, advancements in leaf color, texture and form will make this your favorite garden specimen. With very low inputs required

– meaning low fertility, limited insect pressure, and low water needs – hazelnuts are the perfect landscape plant. They can be grown as a screen, border or single specimen, though I can't imagine having only one tree! Hardy in USDA zones 3-8, this small tree offers huge opportunities for homesteaders, local foodies and residential gardeners.

The colorful husks add mid-summer interest and the nuts will drop to the ground when ripe. Adored by all creatures, especially squirrels, its benefits will be reaped by only the most attentive harvesters. The nuts develop their signature flavor after a short roast in a warm oven. The nuts are ideal for candies, cakes and other sweet treats, and can also be processed into oil of high culinary value.

Colorful husks add interest to the landscape.

PECANS (*Carya illinoinensis*)

I have often said "the best pecan is planted in your neighbor's yard" because pecans do come with some disadvantages, including the softwood nature of this tree, which results in frequent and random branch loss. However, I argue that the value of these long-lived specimens outranks the trouble. From the distinctly delicious flavor of the nuts to the incredible buttery-yellow fall color of the leaves, pecans are a symbol of the native American flora. Pecan trees are large, so if you have room (and your neighbor doesn't have a tree), it's worth the space.

Grains

This edible meadow features seasonal displays of grains and flowers.

My obsession with growing grains has opened my eyes to a vast array of opportunities to help hyper-localize carbohydrate production in every community through foodscaping. Grains are a vastly under-developed element of the local foods movement. I find myself having to defend the role carbohydrates play in our daily consumption: they're in our diet when we consume them directly or even if we go "low carb" or "paleo." Note to meat-eaters: the diet of most animals you consume consists primarily of grains.

It is my personal opinion that there are a lot of untruths circulating about the role grains play in the human diet. For instance, society has evolved for more than 7,000 years because of the cultivation of wheat. Yes, wheat is responsible for the creation of community. It was the caloric intake that this crop provided that enabled human beings to develop specialized skills that we now recognize as civilized society and the ability to stay in one place.

In the past 30 years of biotech-heavy commercial agriculture, we've seen a rapid evolution of modern breeding and the chemistry culture (with little awareness by most of us). This could be a cause for the recent spike in gluten intolerances and dietary problems associated with grains. It is this very reason that the local foods movement must address the growing of carbohydrate sources in a more ethical, nutritious manner.

Grains are the edible equivalents of ornamental grasses, full of seasonal appeal and biodiversity. They can be used in mass plantings for edible meadow designs or grown as clumps for a formal aesthetic. The beauty and utility that common grains offer will change your perspective forever. Grains deserve a spot in every single landscape because they are practical pillars of our everyday consumption, and with unmatched curb appeal. I think grains are the "gateway plant" for getting edibles into more commercial landscapes.

AMARANTH (Amaranthus spp.)

I am new to growing amaranth. Admittedly, I have stayed away from it because of the seeding reputation it has. I figured if I was growing it to harvest the seed, that shouldn't be a problem; time will tell if I have unleashed my next headache.

I foolishly sowed this grain as a cool season crop, and was so disappointed that the seed sat dormant while my cool season grains happily grew. But then the soil temperatures rose to 60°F and suddenly there was a groundcover visible overnight. Realizing my mistake, I took some time to thin the seedlings into a mid-border area of my foundation landscape.

To say the least, the amaranth grew with vigor to over 6' tall and set MILLIONS of seeds. Amaranth has been growing for thousands of years in warm

climates as an important, gluten-free carbohydrate source. As more people become afflicted with gluten intolerances, crops such as quinoa and amaranth offer a significant solution.

This may not be an ideal specimen for every landscape. My plants suffered severe foliage damage from various beetles and the plants grew way out of scale. However, in a property screen amaranth would be a great seasonal edible solution that looks nice mingled with conifers and flowering shrubs, and is sure to hide your neighbor's lot.

BARLEY (Hordeum vulgare)

The influence of home brewing has inspired a renaissance of grains, including in the foodscape. Barley is just one grain that can be used in brewing beer and is an outstanding plant for the spring landscape. Like other cool season grains, barley will germinate in cool soils. I sow after Thanksgiving for a spring harvest, but in cooler climates late winter sowing is recommended.

Barley will germinate quickly and resemble "grass" while it stretches to the sky and ultimately develops a seed head that is very similar to wheat. Hand harvest when the stalks turn beige and thresh by tapping seed heads against the side of a bucket. It's a process, but if nothing else, you will get some bragging rights for taking the home brewing hobby to a new level of homesteading!

Amaranth is a vigorous grower and will set millions of seeds on one plant.

BUCKWHEAT (*Fagopyrum esculentum*)

Buckwheat was recommended to me by Dr. Dennis Werner of NCSU as an ideal summer cover crop to increase populations of beneficial pollinators and add organic matter to the soil. I was impressed by the almost instant germination rate and rapid growth. Within 20 days the plants were covered in brilliant white flowers that played host to countless varieties of native bees, wasps and butterflies.

The seed set is abundant and the plants will naturalize in an area if allowed to self sow. The ease of growing and beautiful flowers are reason enough to sprinkle seed and allow the buckwheat magic to happen. I was curious about the culinary use of buckwheat, so I gathered seed and hand ground it into a dark flour-like substance, which is perfect for making buckwheat pancakes.

Now I can't imagine how I lived a happy life without this cheerful cover crop in my mix. No landscape or garden is complete without buckwheat. The easy-to-grow, full-sun nature of this pollinator magnet makes it a must.

OATS (*Avena sativa*)

Perhaps the most beautiful of the common grains, oats have a taller, more open structure than, say, rice. Topping out at 4-5' tall when the seed is ripe, oats are an elegant addition to a property border and look great against an evergreen backdrop. I prefer to grow oats as thick clumps, which makes hand harvesting much easier. I start the seed in communal flats in mid-October (late winter in colder climates) and plant the clumps on "Black Friday" (I always choose to garden the day after Thanksgiving and avoid the chaos of disposable shopping. My friends and family seem to prefer meaningful homegrown gifts, anyway).

The foliage is a lovely silver-blue color and is much wider in comparison to wheat or barley. Oats have strong cold tolerance and remain evergreen in my Carolina foodscape through single-digit lows and occasional snow and ice cover.

The plants will grow with vigor as the spring season begins to warm up, and by Mother's Day the seed is starting to set.

Harvesting and threshing by hand is an experience that every person should have just to appreciate what the Quaker Oats Company provides; we take the accessibility of food for granted. The seed will pop out of the chaff easily after a few "beatings" against a board positioned inside a bucket. There are hull-less selections available in the marketplace to help reduce the labor. The seed can then be soaked, dry stored or frozen, ready for your next hearty breakfast.

Rice is ready to harvest when the kernals are plump and begin bending the plant stems.

RICE (Oryza sativa)

My very favorite summer crop, rice, just may be the catalyst for the Foodscape Revolution. It is the perfect substitution for the annual "fountain grasses" that grace every planter and entryway in commercial landscapes. Unlike the floppy ornamental grasses, rice has incredible structural integrity, sets edible seed for an extended season, and grows happily with the same irrigation cycle as most ornamentals. There are many varieties of rice available, including purple or yellow foliage forms. The green selections have great vigor and abundant seed set.

Most people assume rice has to be grown in water. The truth is that "upland" varieties of rice are well adapted to growing in many soil conditions. The flooding of rice patties was originally started as a means of natural weed control but is not necessary for growing upland varieties in the home landscape.

Rice is a warm season crop and should be started in communal trays (see page 57) in the warmth of a home or greenhouse. After the threat of frost, clumps of rice can be transplanted into the landscape. These will grow through the summer into 3-4' specimens with long drooping seed heads that are attractive and, most importantly, harvestable!

Threshing is easy: simply heat a pan or wok with no oil and stir the seed stalks. The seed will pop out of the chaff and be ready for culinary use just like the rice you buy at the store. I store my homegrown rice in the the freezer to ensure freshness. It is too easy to grow not to try at least once. The handsome form and easy-to-use edible component will leave you smitten, just like me.

RYE *(Secale cereale)*

Rye is a grass grown as a grain, cover crop, and/or a livestock forage crop throughout the world. It is closely related to barley and wheat, and is used to make flour, whiskey and vodka. You can eat it whole, either as boiled rye berries or after it has been rolled, which would taste similar to rolled oats. Rye is a cereal with a large seed. Do not confuse it with ryegrass, which is commonly used to enhance cool season lawns.

Rye is best grown in full sun and nutrient-rich soil. I like to grow it in clumps. I sow the seed in late summer in communal trays and transplant "pinches" of the plants (small groups) into my cool season landscape. Much like wheat and barley, rye will overwinter and then begin to grow with vigor as the cool soil warms to above 50°F. As the day length increases, the plants will develop handsome flower stalks and ultimately will dry to a dark brown.

Growing rye is an experience of beauty, bounty and historical significance, and rye is a novel crop to produce without the aid of mechanized harvesting and processing equipment. The ancient grains are glorious ambassadors of the spring landscape and are just as beautiful as ornamental grasses — if not more so.

SESAME *(Sesamum indicum)*

Sesame is cultivated for its edible seeds that develop abundantly in pods along the 6'-tall flower stalks. In 2013, 4.2 million metric tons of sesame seeds were harvested globally. I originally got a pack of seed from Monticello. With no expectations, I sowed the seed in a sunny summer border and was shocked by how enamored I became with this plant.

Sesame plants are gorgeous and easy to grow from seed directly sown in the landscape, so I simply do not understand why they aren't more widely available. With velvety green foliage and white, foxglove-like flowers that bloom through the heat of the summer, sesame is as beautiful as it is functional.

Native to India, sesame is tolerant of drought-like conditions. It is one of the oldest oilseed crops known, domesticated well over 3,000 years ago, and has one of the highest oil contents of any seed. With a rich, nutty flavor, it is a common ingredient in cuisines across the world. This is an edible that needs to be in every landscape because it is beautiful, bountiful and just strange enough to make people ask questions. You can easily grow enough sesame to meet your needs; in fact, you'll probably find yourself incorporating it into many more dishes when you have your own and don't have to buy expensive jars of it at the store.

The seeds are harvested by cutting the dry stalk and turning it upside-down in a bucket or brown bag. Toast in a warm oven, press to make oil, or refrigerate for fresh, raw sesame seed, which can be sown the following summer.

SORGHUM (Sorghum bicolor)

Native to Africa, cane and grain sorghum is a global staple, ranking as the the fifth most important cereal crop in the world. It is also used in the production of alcoholic beverages and biofuels, but I prefer to grow cane sorghum as a local, sustainable sugar source. There are, however, some processing impracticalities. Without a sorghum press, extracting the sugary liquid from the canes is very difficult. My husband purchased a small, hand crank press for me from Amazon. It arrived from Japan and works great, and my forearms are strong from processing our fall crop! Grain sorghum is a beautiful addition to the landscape and is a host to

a wide variety of beneficial insects. This is easily harvested and can be ground into flour or distributed to hungry birds throughout the winter.

The high drought and heat tolerance of sorghum make this an ideal candidate for those who live in hot climates throughout the southeast and southwest U.S. Seed germinates easily when sown directly into the landscape in clumps. Thumb 3-5 seeds 2" deep into the ground and cover with a light layer of mulch. Plants will germinate within a week in warm soil and will quickly develop into tall stalks with gorgeous seed heads.

Sorghum has become my favorite edible of the summer for its dark green foliage, attractive screening size, and the pollinator habitat it creates. Aphids may invade the underside of the foliage in mid-summer, but allow the naturally occurring ecological system to balance this infestation. The "honeydew" dropping from the aphids will attract a diverse range of beneficial insects, and ladybug larvae will feast on the undesired pests.

WHEAT *(Triticum aestivum)*

Wheat is a winter crop in my zone 7 region, but in cooler climates, some varieties can be planted in early spring to ripen in summer. You can grow it from seed and there are many varieties, both modern and ancient, to choose from. The advantages of growing ancient varieties are vast. They are easier to digest, growing them is an effective way to preserve germplasm (the living genetic tissue), and the seed of ancient varieties can be removed from the hull through hand threshing. However, modern cultivars boast improvements in disease resistance and structural integrity. I recommend growing a few varieties of each so you can compare the difference.

Admittedly, growing wheat is the easy part. Without mechanization it can be a laborious process to harvest, thresh and grind. However, wheat as a landscape plant checks all of the value boxes. It is an inexpensive, low-maintenance, easy-to-grow seasonal annual. Wheat provides great winter interest and is aesthetically pleasing, in addition to its edible component. The dried amber-colored stalks are perfect for flower arrangements and make a unique gift, providing ample reason to grow a few clumps and not dive into the processing at all.

Wheat seed will germinate either in the ground directly or in communal flats for transplanting, to create the clump-like look of an ornamental grass. Add an organic fertilizer at the time of sowing to provide all of the nutrients for the 6-7-month growing season. Germination will occur within 14 days and the bright green new growth will look just like grass – because wheat is a grass in the Poaceae family! Newly sprouted wheat seed is also called cat grass, and you will often find neighborhood kitties grazing your patch.

You will know when it's harvest season because the plants will flower and turn amber. In my climate, this occurs just as the comfortable spring temperatures rise to over 95°F, driving me outside to hand harvest bundles at 6:00 am, before the sun rises. Threshing is the next labor-intensive process, which includes beating the stalks against a hard surface and collecting the seed as it becomes dislodged. To remove the chaff, pour the seed into an empty bucket with a box fan blowing. The heavy seed will fall into the bucket while all of the lightweight materials such as stems and chaff will blow away. *Note:* Be sure to save some whole seed for sowing the following season, and always store seed in the refrigerator (not freezer).

Grinding the seed into flour is the next step for consumption. There are hand crank grinders available and attachments for mixers such as Kitchen Aid. One trick I have discovered is to use a coffee grinder – great for making small batches of freshly ground flour for tortillas. Remember, this is unbleached flour. I recommend storing the flour in the freezer to ensure freshness and quality.

I encourage everyone I meet to consider investing a few dollars in grain seed. Grain can be designed into landscapes in multiple ways. For those who are attracted to mixed meadow plantings, sow the seed directly into the landscape with other flowering plants such as poppies, larkspur and nigella. If you desire a more formal look, sow the seed in communal flats, then pluck out clumps and plant them in staggered groupings, as you would plant an ornamental grass. The clumps will mature into lovely 3'-tall specimens that can add seasonal interest to any border.

Six

FOODSCAPE BASIC CARE & MAINTENANCE

THE BEAUTY OF A FOODSCAPE the way I grow it is that it's pretty low maintenance. You'll do a substantial re-plant of seasonal edibles twice a year, which is the most labor-intensive part. However, make no mistake: growing this much of your own food is definitely a lifestyle choice and you will have to spend some time on it – just not as much time as you might think. In this chapter I'm offering some basics for foodscape care and maintenance. Issues and questions beyond the scope of this chapter can be addressed at your garden center or online, or with your local Cooperative Extension office.

Soil Testing

Allow me to remind you to get a yearly soil test every other year or so. That way you can head off problems before they surface. See some specifics about soil testing on page 37.

Fertilizing

I like to add an organic fertilizer to the soil when I'm planting. There are many different name brands available: Plant-tone® and the GrowScripts product line are just two among many. This will feed the soil microbes and result in healthier plants over time. These slow-release or, more accurately, "slow to break down," organic types of fertilizer will provide enough nutrition for your plants during their growing season, provided that you started by adding a good layer of compost (see page 51) on top of the planting area.

Water with liquid organic fertilizer, like fish emulsion, every three weeks or so. This is a great way to feed containers. Check the labels of the fertilizer you're using to make sure you're not overdosing fruiting plants such as tomatoes, zucchini and eggplants on nitrogen (N), which can cause lots of vegetative growth but no fruit set. Containers do require more frequent feeding than landscape beds because nutrients tend to wash out through frequent waterings.

Alternative growing systems (i.e., hydroponics, aeroponics and aquaponics) have their own requirements. See page 147 for information about how to fertilize plants in those systems.

Watering

You'll have to water seeds and plants most frequently while they're sprouting or establishing new roots. The soil should generally be about as moist as a wrung-out sponge – not sopping wet but not bone dry either. Before watering, check the soil moisture with your fingers. You'll get used to learning when plants need water and when they don't.

When watering by hand, I like to use a hose and watering wand with a breaker on the end. The watering wand helps me extend my reach and place the stream of water exactly where I want it: at the plants' roots. The breaker helps reduce the intensity of the water spray so that it doesn't

Praise for
Brie Arthur *and* The Foodscape Revolution

"Brie Arthur is my go-to expert for all things foodscaping. Her experience, talent and passion for designing edible landscapes is second to none. I'm constantly amazed by Brie's ability and vision for making any plantable space attractive and productive. "

~ **Joe Lamp'l,** Producer and Host of Growing a Greener World®

"*The Foodscape Revolution* is aimed to empower people living in neighborhoods with outdated HOA restrictions that say 'no food in the front yard.' Brie Arthur's design strategy is a way to follow the rules while making the most of the landscape that exists."

~ **Rosalind Creasy,** author of *Edible Landscaping* and *Recipes from the Garden*

"The term 'revolution' is used far too casually today. Very seldom do we see a trend become a movement, then become part of our vocabulary. Brie Arthur has not only been the leader of the foodscape revolution, she is also its face and voice. This is one book that needed to be written."

~ **Allan M. Armitage,** Professor Emeritus of Horticulture, University of Georgia

"Few garden movements have combined the burgeoning desire of people to take control of their food sources while still creating beautiful and functional garden spaces, even as our landscapes are shrinking. Brie is leading the way in the foodscape revolution with bounteous borders of vegetables and flowering perennials, grains and showy shrubs – and she makes it all seem so easy."

~ **Mark Weathington,** Director, JC Raulston Arboretum at NC State University

"This book ushers in a new era of gardening – one where beauty and food grow side-by-side and creativity is not just appreciated, it's encouraged. *The Foodscape Revolution* shows us how to make our landscape sing!"

~ **Jessica Walliser,** horticulturist, radio host, and author of *Attracting Beneficial Bugs to Your Garden* and *Good Bug Bad Bug*

"No longer must food gardening be relegated to a separate part of the garden and ornamentals and flowers to a foundation planting. In *The Foodscape Revolution*, Brie invites us to join her cause: marrying all plant types together as one big happy family, with the homeowner being the recipient of all its glorious bounty."

~ **Maria Zampini,** President, UpShoot LLC

"Brie Arthur transformed her own yard into a beautiful edible haven. Now, she urges us to consider how much food can be grown in the open mulched spaces in our own yards – or on school campuses, in parks, outside office buildings, senior centers and new housing developments.

~ **Ira Wallace,** Southern Exposure Seed Exchange, author of *The Timber Press Guide to Vegetable Gardening in the Southeast*

"Read just a few pages of this exciting new book and you will be energized to try new things in the garden – like, why not use lettuce as an edging or grains as a 'thriller' component? It makes so much sense to do away with the old notion of keeping your edible garden in the backyard."

~ **Diane Blazek,** Executive Director, National Garden Bureau

"Brie Arthur's foodscaping wisdom and creativity shine through in this indispensable book. Integrating edibles with ornamental plants maximizes the purpose of cultivating the Earth in such a way that aids our species in lasting into the indefinite future."

~ **Will Hooker,** Professor Emeritus, NC State Department of Horticulture and Certified PINA Permaculture Designer and Teacher

"In *The Foodscape Revolution*, you will discover a cornucopia of ideas to transform your garden into an edible wonderland! You'll be inspired by seeing the impact that foodscaping can have on your life, your community and your environment."

~ **Jared Barnes,** Ph.D., Professor at Stephen F. Austin State University

"Thanks to Brie Arthur, our school garden at Dorothy L. Bullock Elementary School has become a foodscape haven for the children and residents of Glassboro, New Jersey. Through Brie's devotion to helping our children fall in love with gardening, our innovative programs have been recognized by the NJ Department of Agriculture and won the very first Jersey Fresh Farm-to-School award. Bullock Children's Garden has become a model for other schools."

~ **Sonya Harris,** Special Educator & Lead Coordinator of The Bullock Children's Garden/Glassboro Public Schools Garden Initiative

I scatter a slow-release organic fertilizer over the landscape bed as I plant.

dislodge plants from their planting holes or seeds from the garden bed.

For containers, I like a long-neck watering can with a breaker on the end of the spout. The long neck helps me reach containers that are higher up, such as hanging baskets. Of course, you can water hanging baskets with a watering wand as well, but if you're watering with fish emulsion, you'll need to mix it in a watering can. And take care not to get it on yourself. It's stinky!

Sprinklers are great for watering large beds, though they're less efficient, in terms of water placement. Don't use sprinklers on windy days, as the water will end up everywhere but in the soil. As described in Chapter One, once the plants are established, you'll water plants in foodscape Zone 3 much less than plants in Zones 2 and 1, all things being equal.

Some edibles need more water or more consistent water than others. Follow the lists in Chapter One that describe what to plant and where, to simplify watering the foodscape.

Staking & Supporting

It is by far easier to place plant stakes and supports when you plant than after the fact. If you try to wrestle a full-grown tomato into a cage, you'll break off half of the limbs. Smaller bush-like plants don't need to be staked. I'm always in favor of letting vining plants ramble up trees and shrubs in the foodscape to further reinforce the intermingling of edibles and ornamentals. Following are my tips for staking plants in the foodscape.

Staking materials for large and/or vining plants

Stake indeterminate tomatoes, squash vines, cucumbers and pole beans with…

- **Tomato cages**
- **Concrete reinforcing wire**
- **Cattle fence**

Staking materials for bush-type edibles

Stake bush-type tomatoes, peppers, eggplants and smaller edibles with…

- **Tomato cages**
- **Single stakes**

Not all plants need to be staked; in fact, most do not. Greens, root vegetables, peanuts, soybeans, bush-type beans, bush-type cucumbers and grains all do just fine on their own.

Winter squash growing through a 'Limelight' hydrangea.

Weeding

The way you plant the foodscape has a lot to do with the weed problems you will face. By spreading mulch after sowing you'll prevent many weed seeds from sprouting. I also tend to sow edibles thickly so that they outcompete the weeds. For the most part, I don't sweat the weeds. When I see them, I pull them. Sometimes I let them get pretty big before I pull them. They're easier to see that way.

Controlling Pests and Diseases

Contrary to what chemical companies would have you believe, it is unlikely that you're going to have to wage and all-out war against garden pests and diseases. Depending on where you live and the particular problems of your yard, there may be some serious, isolated issues to overcome, but there's an organic, earth-friendly way around almost everything.

For example, I have terrible problems with root knot nematodes, a common issue in the Southeast. I can't grow tomatoes, cucmbers and melons in the ground, so I've switched to alternative growing systems, outlined in Alternative Growing Systems starting on page 141. If you're having specific problems with only one type of plant or plants in the same family – strange leaf color or anemic growth – look for contextual clues to help you figure out what might be going on. My neighborhood and garden is on the site of an old tobacco farm, and root knot nematodes infect all the soil. I recognizie this because of my education and experience in horticulture, but too many other

Caterpillar on amaranth

Caterpillar on lettuce

Cabbage dusted with Bt

home gardeners don't realize that this soil-borne problem is not the cause of their "black thumb." And though the nematodes are here to stay, they're not insurmountable.

Really, I hate to use the word pest because even the organisms that we would consider problematic have a benefit for some other creature. The point of foodscaping is that you look at the landscape as a biological system or ecosystem that includes a diverse variety of food plants, ornamentals and natives. A diverse landscape is generally able to keep itself in balance. Additionally, because you're likely to plant the same edible in multiple places in the landscape, it's unlikely that you would lose the entire crop from the same problem.

When you spray or control for one out-of-balance pest you risk disrupting the entire system and actually causing more problems. Chemical control applications must be the absolute last resort. Cultural solutions, such as growing tomatoes in soil-less water systems to avoid root knot nematodes altogether, are much better for achieving your desired result – a balanced ecosystem and a healthy, organically cultivated harvest.

Bottom line: it is easy to blame big, commercial agriculture for environmental problems caused by chemical runoff and to not think about the space we're living in every day. The suburban landscape covers a lot of acreage, and small changes to the way we manage these spaces can have a big impact on the environment.

You will encounter issues from time to time and I don't want you to give up because you don't know what to do. If you're finding that a plant is continuously underperforming, get a soil test and a plant materials sample test. The results will shed light on why a tomato suddenly dies or why a plant isn't producing enough fruit. Soil and materials tests are done through your local Cooperative Extension office. For a materials test, you'll send a part of the affected plant along with the paperwork (see page 37).

Some Common Problems and Where to Look for Solutions

Mammals

Mammals can be one of the biggest problems, usually by eating your harvest before you get to. Luckily, non-chemical controls are the most effective against mammals – specifically, barriers. Though not always aesthetically pleasing, barriers such as electric fencing, netting, underground fencing and row covers work well to help break the pattern of browsing. Mammals are creatures of habit, and you can install temporary barriers to "re-train" the animals and successfully reduce the damage long-term. For landscape use, electric fencing around larger bits of property can deter deer. Black netting when a harvest is ripening can protect fruit from chipmunks, rabbits and other animals, including birds! Repellent sprays that make plants taste and smell unfavorable are also available, and are very useful when applied frequently. They might have to be reapplied after a rainstorm, and you have to change products every few months, as the pests will acclimate to the smell and taste. One of my favorite methods to stop mammals from entering your foodscape is installing a motion-detecting sprinkler system. This is an effective way to scare off mammals such as deer and water your garden at the same time.

Insects

Insects are a vital part of our ecosystems and our garden health. They're pollinators, which are responsible for one out of every three bites

This tomato hornworm is infested with parasitic wasp eggs - which will eventually kill the host hornworm.

of food we take. Insects are food for birds and food for each other. To try to eradicate them, wholesale, from the garden is not only impractical, it's dangerous. That is not what "gardening" commercials on television would lead you to believe, though. Let me tell you – a hole from a bug is not the end of the world. But having no insects in the garden most definitely *could* be.

When you plant your foodscape as a diverse ecosystem you will encounter fewer issues with insects. Of course there will some occasions when a population will be disruptive enough that you'll need to do something about them. Beware of broad-spectrum pesticides that kill everything that moves. Use the least invasive control methods first and work your way up. The whole point of this management strategy of foodscaping is to be organically driven. I prefer to use soft chemistries and oils to deal with out-of-control insects like aphids, which will attack new growth, or tea scale, which can cover the backside of broad leaf evergreens, like camellias. Horticultural, dormant and neem oils are very helpful in smothering problem bugs and not impacting the entire balance of the ecosystem.

Caterpillars such as squash vine borer and cabbage worms can be controlled with *Bacillus thuringiensis*, or *Bt*. This is quite effective and completely organic. Japanese beetles can lay waste to edibles and ornamentals, but don't use traps, because the traps will actually lure in more beetles. Birds can help control Japanese beetles. If you see tomato hornworms (they're big green worms the size of your thumb), pick them off and allow the wasps, who are the good guys here, to parasitize the hornworms. Aphids can be a common problem on edibles and ornamentals. You can try blasting them off of the plants with water or letting the other beneficial insects work their magic and eat the aphids. There are a few edibles you just won't be able to grow without controlling the pests (cabbage worms are one), but in most cases, if you're prepared to lose a few plants here and there you'll be fine gardening without intervention.

Nematodes

Tomatoes, carrots, figs and many root vegetables are susceptible to root knot nematodes. One cultural measure you can use to control nematodes is to grow a bunch of marigolds to mow over and plow under into the soil. This is a short-term approach; you can also grow plants in soil-filled containers or hydroponics.

Bacterial, Fungal and Viral Diseases

There are a myriad of bacterial, fungal and viral diseases that affect plants. The first line of defense is to plant resistant varieties when you can find them. Resistance is marked on the seed packet. For instance, "TMV" indicates resistance to tobacco mosaic virus, while "CMV" would indicate resistance to cucumber mosaic virus. To help cope with soil-borne diseases, rotate crops or grow in containers, switching out the soil each growing season.

Root knot nematodes on okra roots

Identifying and Correcting Cultural Problems

If a plant isn't performing at peak, it might not be an insect or pest problem causing it. Cultural problems – issues with the environment in which the plant is growing – are responsible for plenty of gardening fails. Nutrient deficiencies usually show themselves as discolored leaves. A soil test and/or a materials test can help you identify those. In hydroponics, nutrient deficiencies show up almost instantly when the solutions are off-balance. Read more about that in Alternative Growing Systems starting on page 141.

Common Problems with Tomatoes and Peppers

1: Blossom end rot

Tomatoes and peppers exhibit symptoms of blossom end rot. That can be a water or soil pH problem or a water amount problem. Calcium

deficiency causes blossom end rot in soils that are too acidic because acid blocks calcium uptake. A wet/dry/wet/dry sequence of soil moisture can also cause problems with blossom end rot.

Blossom end rot on tomato

2. Cracking fruit

Cracking is caused by plants receiving too much water followed by not enough. Consistency of care is key in preventing that cultural problem.

3: Flower drop and a lull in fruit production

This often happens during mid-summer in warm climates. In areas of extreme heat, you can replant two crops of tomatoes.

As you grow your foodscape, you'll learn which problems you need to worry about and solve, and which are simply cosmetic and don't require your time. There's a wealth of region-specific information available online and in bookstores about garden care and maintenance that can further help you increase your bounty. Experience with your garden soil and climate is also an amazing teacher. Enjoy the process!

Part Two:

FOODSCAPING PROJECTS

Let's kick it up a notch: Now that you've got the
foodscape basics down, what about putting that
knowledge to work with a few lifestyle-enhancing
projects? In this section I'll show you some designs
and planting suggestions that you can use or
adapt to your specific space and taste.

FOODIE FIRE PIT
A four-season gathering space

I started designing "foodie fire pits" because, while most people dream of that campfire moment, frequently the space goes unused. To build an entire garden room for a fire pit, complete with seating, hardscape, and the fire element itself, can cost as much as ten thousand and fifteen thousand dollars. That's a lot of money for an area that doesn't otherwise see daily action.

However, when you design with edibles, the space becomes useful year-round and there is an additional reason to interact in the space. Come on out! The foodie fire pit serves as a great gathering place during the summer, even when your first thought might not be "let's huddle around a blazing hot fire." (Unless, of course, you live in the arctic north.) A fire pit is one of the few outdoor gathering spaces without a central table. It is an area that encourages relaxation and fun. We love sitting around ours, even in the summer, because we can reach out and snack on the nearby blueberries while we're chatting with friends.

A happy accident led to my foodie fire pit – in the form of the cover. A living wall garden that my husband built didn't work where we intended it to go, but it turned out the perfect size to use as a cover for the otherwise empty hole in the center of our entertainment space. In the winter, we plant the 2" depth of soil in the cover with lettuce and greens, and in the summer it's celosia. The celosia doesn't grow very tall, but the spiky red flowers do look like "flames," even when the fire isn't burning.

Shrub Framework

People like fire pits to feel cozy and enclosed. Accomplish this by creating a garden room using ornamental and edible shrubs, groundcovers and edging. Don't feel like you have to go hard on the edibles. My foodie fire pit has a hedge of blueberries, but if you don't need or want 8 or 10 blueberry bushes, you could plant a hedge of azaleas or other mid-sized flowering shrubs with a blueberry bush on either side of the entryway. For this project, shrubs that stay compact or respond well to hedging are ideal framework plants.

Fire pits are great areas for alternative growing systems that require power because there's almost always electricity around them. Along one side of our foodie fire pit, I grow 10'-tall hydroponic tomatoes, which form a wall of foliage with easy access to harvest ripe fruit.

Edible

- Apple Tree, espaliered (sometimes available pre-trained)
- Asparagus
- Blueberry
- *Camellia sinensis* ("tea shrub")
- Fig
- Hazelnut/Filbert
- Persimmon Tree

Ornamental

It's helpful to choose ornamentals with similar soil requirements (moisture and pH, particularly) as the edibles. For example, azaleas and hollies grow well with blueberries because they all thrive in acidic soil.

- Abelia
- Azalea
- Boxwood
- Camellia
- Holly
- Rose
- Spiraea
- Taxus
- Weigela
- Yew

Edible Ambience

In addition to the permanent ornamental/edible framework of shrubs, you can enjoy seasonal edibles planted as groundcovers, edging, and even as one side of the garden "room." Note the big hydroponic tomatoes that form a backdrop behind the "couch" next to my fire pit. In the winter this is replaced with large containers of hardy greens like arugula, kale and Swiss chard. My clothesline is on the other side of the fire pit "room." In the summer, when it is too humid to air-dry anything, I let cucumber, squash and gourd vines scramble up and across the lines. Then, in the winter, the lines are free for drying blankets.

Groundcovers & Edging

Flowering perennials and low-maintenance groundcovers are fantastic! Summer bloomers like phlox, echinacea and rudbeckia mingle perfectly with strawberries as a groundcover. Peanuts, peppers, lettuce and garlic are ideal edging plants to extend the purpose of the space.

Perennials

- Creeping Jenny
- Oregano
- **Strawberries** *(I love the new pink-flowered ever-bearing varieties.)*
- Thyme

Cool Season

- Arugula
- Garlic
- Kale
- Lettuce
- Onion
- Swiss Chard

Warm Season

- Basil
- Peanut
- Pepper
- **Soybean** *(for edamame)*
- Squash
- Sweet Potato
- Zucchini

Blueberries have great fall color.

Foodie fire pits can be as formal or informal as you choose. Unless steep slopes are present where load bearing walls would need to be constructed, no permits or engineering are required. Consider the hardscape materials first: there are many options, from loose gravel to brick or pavers as a foundation. Also, determine how much square footage needs to be devoted to the space by identifying how many seats will circle the pit. Finally, decide how large and what shape it should be and select a complementary, fire-resistant material for construction. Remember, fire needs to breathe in order to burn efficiently. A wider opening and

lower profile (24-28" deep) will allow for proper airflow, which will keep your foodie fire pit aglow for hours.

Prepare the Soil

Soil prep is important for all gardens, but particularly so if you're going to plant a hedge of blueberries. They require acidic conditions and moist, loamy soil. If you live in an area with a naturally high soil pH, look for organic soil acidifier products, many of which will include aluminum sulfate. Amend the soil with ground pine bark before planting, and add at least 6" of compost on top of the area where you plan to plant.

Plant the Edible & Ornamental Shrub Framework

Once the hardscape (fire pit and patio) is complete, start by placing and planting the ornamental and edible shrubs that will be the framework of the garden room. Keep in mind the eventual mature size of the plants. They might be small to start, but they will grow into a hedge.

Add Perennial & Seasonal Edibles

You'll have more room for seasonal edibles when you first plant the framework around the foodie fire pit. The shrubs will grow and eventually take over more space in the landscape beds. Until then, groundcovers like sweet potatoes and squash will come in handy to keep the weeds down and make the open mulch space productive.

Growing the Foodie Fire Pit

As with any foodscape, the growing season is regionally timed and harvests will be influenced by temperatures and rainfall. By selecting a diverse range of ornamental and edible plants, your foodie fire pit will boast year-round interest, value and bounty.

Fertilize shrubs in the spring and fall with appropriate fertilizer for the shrub. I always dig in a general-purpose organic fertilizer such as Plant-tone when I plant seasonal edibles.

Prune spring-flowering ornamental shrubs after they bloom. Prune summer-flowering shrubs in the winter or early spring. Prune blueberries mid-summer as new growth develops. Blueberries fruit on "old" (or last season's) wood, so avoid hard cutbacks by managing the size throughout the growing season.

Harvest as fruits ripen to keep the plants productive. Clip individual leaves of Swiss chard and kale starting from the outside and working in. Cut-and-come-again lettuce can be sheared daily for salads.

Eat up!

Grilled asparagus: Put asparagus in a bag with salt, pepper, chopped garlic, and olive oil. Massage that so it coats the asparagus. You can grill it or steam it on the stovetop, depending on how crunchy you want it to be.

Open-faced fig sandwich: Slice figs in half. Spread hearty crusty bread with goat cheese, top with arugula and fig halves. Toast until cheese starts to bubble.

This 850 square foot bed dissects the middle of the front yard providing seasonal screening.

PROPERTY SCREEN MEADOW
You can have a meadow and eat it, too

Along the highways in North Carolina, large sweeps of wildflowers — sunflowers and cosmos, poppies and cornflowers — break up what is otherwise a never-ending landscape of pine trees. Those splashes of seasonal flowers inspired this project: a blending of edibles (grains, herbs and vegetables) with ornamentals to create a useful and beautiful property screen with minimal inputs. It offers a prairie look without the expense of purchasing three-gallon ornamental grass plants. I tried that one time, spending roughly $600 on native pink muhly grass. When it all died during a particularly soggy winter, I took Ros Creasy's advice and started over with grains. Grains are just as beautiful as their ornamental relatives, but more useful, less expensive (you plant seed instead of potted plants), and easier to maintain. Remember, plants sown in place set deeper roots, which makes them more tolerant of drought and better able to out-compete weeds.

Our meadow winds through the center of our front yard, screening our front porch from the street. It is surrounded by carefully-tended turf, which keeps the HOA happy. You can easily adapt this project to property line beds, as well, on any size or scale — mine is about 850 square feet. Because different plants grow well in winter or the cool season than in the summer or warm season, growing a meadow will allow you to experience dramatic seasonal changes. The varied mixture of plant types creates a biodiverse ecosystem, which keeps pest and disease problems to a minimum. This natural look mimics nature while providing your family with nourishment.

Grow It!

Wheat and larkspur

Winter or cool season meadow:

- Barley
- Carrot
- Cilantro
- Larkspur
- Nigella
- Poppy
- Rye
- Wheat

Scatter these seeds thickly, spacing them ½ - 1½" apart. Sow as if you're feeding chickens.

Summer or warm season meadow:

- Basil
- Carrot
- Corn
- Peanut
- Pepper
- Sesame
- Sorghum
- Soybean
- Sunflower
- Zinnia

Thumb seeds of corn, sorghum, sunflowers, soybeans and peanuts into the soil 12" apart. Sow zinnias, basil and sesame as you'd plant the winter seeds, ½ - 1" apart. Transplant peppers from containers to fill in gaps.

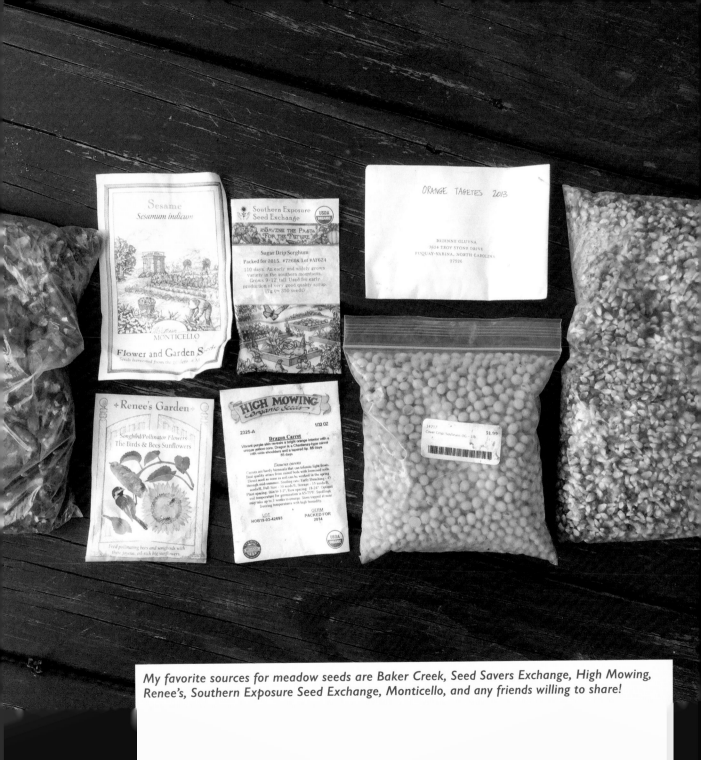

My favorite sources for meadow seeds are Baker Creek, Seed Savers Exchange, High Mowing, Renee's, Southern Exposure Seed Exchange, Monticello, and any friends willing to share!

How to Plant a Meadow

Step 1

Prepare the soil by amending with organic matter or a topdressing with compost. You'll need bare soil on which to scatter the seeds.

Step 2

Mark planting areas with marking paint to ensure the planting will look attractive and organized. It is also easier to harvest grains when they are planted in blocks or blobs, and marking the areas where I want to plant each type makes it easier to quickly sow the seeds. However, this is an optional step. You can also just go with the flow.

Mark planting areas for easy sowing.

Step 3

Sow seed. I sow the seed for the edible meadow one variety at a time. For the winter meadow, I sow the grains such as wheat, oats, barley or rye on the surface of fresh organic matter and rake them in, ensuring good soil contact. On top of the grains I sow flowers and herbs. A good rule of thumb when sowing seeds is to consider the size of the seed. The smaller the seeds, the closer to the surface they need to be sown. For plants such as poppies, larkspur and nigella with dust-like seed, they require light and seasonal freezing and thawing (stratification) to germinate. These are best sown in early winter for spring germination.

The summer meadow requires a slightly more hands-on approach to plant. I start by preparing the bed with a layer of organic matter. Often, I simply layer compost on top of last season's mulch. It is important to sow the seeds when the soil temperature has risen above 65°F, as most warm season crops will not develop in cold soil. I thumb the largest seeds into the soil on 12" spacing, ensuring the design will be cohesive and the plants will have the space to grow to maturity. You can then overseed with filler specimens like zinnia and sesame, and add container-started edibles such as eggplant or peppers for added interest.

Step 4

Mulch. Once the seeds have been sown, you can apply mulch to make the bed look tidy. For the cool season grains meadow, I mulch the outer 12" perimeter of the bed. This cleans the space up and creates a proper edge. For the

Grains sprouting through hardwood mulch.

warm season planting, you can apply a 1-2" layer of hardwood mulch over everything. This will help retain moisture and control weeds. The seedlings will germinate through the mulch within 14 days. I used triple-shredded hardwood because it breaks down fast and adds organic matter to the soil base.

Step 5

Water the seeds. You'll need to water with a sprinkler on a stand once a day for 20 minutes, depending on whether or not you get rain, for the first two weeks. The soil should be moist but not soggy. After a couple of weeks, check the soil moisture a few times a week. If it's dry, water for 20 minutes.

Care & Maintenance

A meadow is the lowest-maintenance edible landscape you can grow! Keep weed problems to a minimum by planting densely and avoiding thinning. Keep it watered until plants are ready to harvest. That's pretty much it.

Sowing a meadow is a great way to get kids involved with gardening!

Ripening wheat

Harvesting & Preserving

You'll know it's time to harvest when everything is so ugly you can't stand to leave it up anymore! First, the grains will turn a golden yellow and everything else will be brown. It is beautiful when it is ripening, but when everything is good and dry, it's time to pull it up, save the seeds and start on the next season.

Use pruners to cut wheat close to the ground in bunches. Rubber-band or tie the bundles and hand thresh. See instructions on page 128.

Harvest carrots as they begin to develop lush foliage and as you are ready to eat them. Allow some plants to go to flower so you can harvest seed and start the cycle over again.

To harvest and save seed for poppies, larkspur, cilantro and sesame, pull the plants and turn them upside down over a bucket to collect seed.

Storage
Store grain in the freezer to avoid spoilage. Roast the peanuts and store in a pantry. Flower seeds are best stored in a plastic container in the refrigerator until the appropriate time to sow again.

EDIBLE NEIGHBORHOOD ENTRYWAY
A simple community garden

I started noticing (and judging) entryway plantings when I was a first-time homeowner paying HOA fees and feeling dissatisfied – particularly with the lackluster professionally-maintained spaces. They're usually not pretty, let alone productive, and they can cost a lot every year. These entryways are present in almost every neighborhood or subdivision, and with money from HOA fees, they could support food production in a beautiful way. Even if there isn't an HOA, many neighborhoods have common spaces and/or landscaped entry signs that could be pressed into service to grow edibles and ornamentals together. Entryways are easy places to start if you want to make a difference in your community, because you live close by and can easily maintain it. From the edible entryway it's easy to extrapolate the same idea to other neighborhood common spaces such as clubhouses – or public spaces such as office parks, schools and municipal parks. It's a matter of thinking about how neighborhoods are allocating the money that they spend and thinking bigger about what their options could be.

In my neighborhood, the kids are the biggest helpers with this space. Really, they're the only people standing around at the entrance to the neighborhood (i.e., the bus stop) for any amount of time, so they take ownership over it. They even pull weeds while they wait for the school bus. Overall, because of the plant selection, it's a low-maintenance area. We might spend eight hours a year, total, working on it. Now, instead of paying landscapers to maintain the space we have a neighborhood party and we get to harvest delicious vegetables from the entry.

They make a nice backdrop for food crops and, if you skip a season with the edibles, the bed will still look tidy and cared for. Plant selection depends on where you live, but generally hollies, azaleas, boxwood, beautyberry, forsythia, itea, roses and ornamental grasses will perform well. Furthermore, this woody ornamental structure can be fertilized less frequently than the seasonal vegetables.

Overstory Trees

If you're foodscaping an island bed, you might be able to skip the evergreen shrubs and go for a few overstory trees. Redbud, crape myrtle, serviceberry, cherry trees and Japanese maples are all good choices. Look for smaller trees that top out at 15-20'. Usually, there are utility lines to contend with in these areas, so you don't want large trees that will get hacked with a chainsaw by utility crews in the future.

Entryways are usually tough sites. They're often not irrigated and have terrible soil. You can amend the soil by adding compost and organic matter, but, in general, you're going to want to select robust plants that aren't affected by road exhaust or fluctuations in moisture. If your neighborhood entry has an island bed in the center, it's also important to think about plant height and visibility when choosing varieties.

Woody Backdrop
(deciduous & evergreen "bones")

Whether the entry bed is an island or a set of signs/beds on either side of the road, flowering and evergreen shrubs are always a good place to start.

Seasonal Selections

I find it easiest to grow more produce during the cool season because infrequent water doesn't bother the plants as much. In the warm season, you can grow peanuts and soybeans without irrigation, both of which also fix nitrogen, preparing the soil for the next season. Annual flowers like sunflowers, zinnias and cleome will tolerate drier conditions, but nearly all other selections may require irrigation during the summer.

Cool Season

Root crops and greens are natural fits for entryway beds because they're fairly tough. Wheat is a beautiful additional for the center of the bed, as it looks like a winter ornamental grass, but gets too tall for clearance near the road. Add poppies and larkspur in with the wheat for extra color and biodiversity.

Edibles

- Beet
- Cabbage
- Carrot
- Collard
- Kale
- Mustard Greens
- Oats
- Parsnip
- Radish
- Rutabaga
- Turnip
- Wheat *(really pretty!)*

Ornamentals

- Calendula
- Larkspur
- Nigella
- Poppy
- Snapdragon
- Viola

Warm Season

Choose plants that are suited to the conditions in the entry bed. If irrigation is available, by all means, take advantage of the space to plant squash, zucchini, melons, eggplants and shorter varieties of peppers. You'll have to pay close attention to zucchini, peppers and eggplants to keep them harvested. If there's no irrigation, go for drought-tolerant flowers (sunflowers, zinnias, and cleome) and nitrogen-fixing edibles, including peanuts and soybeans.

Edibles

- Cantaloupe
- Eggplant
- Peanut
- Pepper
  (that aren't tall)
- Soybean
- Squash
- Tomatillo
- Tomato
- Watermelon
- Zucchini

Ornamentals

- Cleome
- Ginger
- Marigold
- Sunflower
- Zinnia

Planting the Edible Entryway

Prepare soil by adding compost – at least 6". This is the most important step in successfully growing an edible entryway garden. Without supplemental water and tender care for the plants, they're going to rely on what they can get from the soil – nutrients, water and support. Rake in Plant-tone or another organic fertilizer when you spread the compost.

Plant the ornamental framework. With the framework in place first, you'll know how much space you have to plant seasonal edibles and ornamentals. Avoid mid-summer installations in warm climates. Here in North Carolina, I try to plant trees and shrubs in late fall when temperatures are cool and moisture is abundant. Watch the weather forecast and plant when rain is likely to ensure success. Some water may need to be supplemented to get the trees and shrubs established.

Direct sow the seasonal edibles and flowers. I cannot stress enough how important it is to sow seasonal plants directly into the entryway gardens. Plants that have been direct sown are so much more drought tolerant than plugs or transplants and much more likely to survive in beds without irrigation. If the bed is not irrigated, choose plants carefully and watch the forecast so that you can sow the seed a day or so before it looks like you're going to get some rain. The seeds won't germinate until the soil is moist. If I sow seeds and they don't germinate, I will wait and sow again a few weeks

later when the soil is ready. If the bed is irrigated, sow seeds thickly to reduce open space (open space translates to weeds).

Mulch. Adding mulch is an ideal way to reduce weeds, capture moisture and add organic matter to the soil profile while making the bed look clean and tidy. The warm season crops can be mulched over at the time of sowing. Many of the cool season crops, however, need light to germinate; in this case, I recommend waiting to mulch lightly until after the seedlings begin to germinate and grow. While you're waiting, just mulch the edges to help reduce runoff and make the bed look cared for.

Switch out warm season plants for cool season plants and vice versa. Add compost on top of the previous season's mulch, scatter Plant-tone, sow the seeds, and then mulch again.

Care & Harvest

Watering

This space has to survive on its own, with irrigation or rainwater. If the edibles begin to look ratty from lack of hydration, just pull them up and sow fresh seed.

Harvesting

We've been really casual about harvesting. In my neighborhood, adults come out when they see someone else is harvesting. One year at Christmas, the lettuce was so lush they couldn't resist it. A few came out to pick, and a few more, and suddenly the whole neighborhood was there gathering salad greens, turnips and collards for their holiday dinners. I've stood shoulder to shoulder with neighbors who had no idea what all these foods looked like in the ground. They were delighted and so was I!

Weeding

This is really a low-maintenance space. If you get the neighborhood kids involved with planting, they'll usually weed and harvest with some frequency on their own. I work on the entryway bed on Sunday evenings several times through the year, and the children who live at the front of the neighborhood will come out and help. They can teach the other kids.

Eat Up!

Massaged Kale Salad: The best way to eat raw kale is to remove the midrib from the center of the plant, tear it up into 2" pieces, sprinkle some coarse salt and flavored vinegar over it, and scrunch it up with your hands until it starts to soften a bit. Great topped with toasted or raw pumpkin seeds.

PATIO POTS
No yard? No problem!

Anyone with a bit of outdoor space can grow edibles in containers. There are even pint-sized varieties of favorites, like tomatoes, cucumbers and squash, that you wouldn't normally think of planting in pots.

You've probably heard about the three kinds of plants for container designing: *the thriller, the filler* and *the spiller.* The thriller is the largest, most dramatic plant in the mix. The filler fills in with more color and texture, and the spiller drapes itself artfully over the edge. There's no reason why some of these plants can't be edibles. Here are some combination ideas to get you inspired.

Grow It!

Warm Season:

Tomato Tango

The tomato will be the thriller. Tomatoes need steady moisture and good airflow, so take care not to overfill the pot. Pair with calibrachoa or improved petunia; or for a fuller look, some Diamond Frost® euphorbia, which is a good airy filler that won't overwhelm the tomato. Add trailing coleus for the spiller.

Rice, Rice, Baby

Rice plants are grasses, and they look like ornamental grasses in the landscape or containers. Want a conversation starter for your outdoor gatherings? Plant rice in the pots around your patio. Rice plays well with begonias and creeping Jenny.

Eggplant Extravaganza

With proper culture (i.e., good soil, nutrition and regular watering) any variety of eggplant can be used in a mixed container. Select the variety that you like to eat the most, as eggplants can set a lot of fruit! For a dwarf variety, try Patio Baby. Some favorite container friends: Ever Color® carex (sedge) , Diamond Frost® euphorbia, trailing vinca or variegated sweet potato vine.

Pick a Pepper

Peppers are a low-maintenance plant that adds spice and color to patio containers. Since they have the same growing requirements as most other sun-loving, warm-season annuals, you can pair them with just about any plant. Try medium-sized coleus, trailing plectranthus or vinca.

Cucumber Climber

Secure a trellis, tomato cage, or a ring of concrete reinforcing wire in a large whiskey barrel. Plant a couple of cucumbers to climb and two or three sweet potato vines to trail. Both of these plants have high water needs in the summer, so they play well together. Plant one or two medium-sized upright coleus plants near the base of the trellis to hide the bottom of the cucumber and you're good to go.

Edible Window Boxes for Summer

Window boxes can sometimes be challenging to keep watered through the heat of the summer due to container limitations and locations, so I prefer to grow drought tolerant herbs and succulents in my window boxes. Plant things that thrive in dry, poor soil. Some good candidates: carex (sedge), echeveria, lavender, oregano, rosemary, sedum, thyme.

Summer Greens

In northern climes, you can grow lettuce in the summer. In hotter, more humid areas, arugula and Swiss chard are the greens to plant for a vitamin-packed boost. Fill in with a bright torenia flower and add trailing flowering ornamentals like vinca, petunia and calibrachoa (million bells), or flashy trailing foliage varieties like ivy, creeping jenny, plectranthus and sedum.

Cool Season:

Salad Bowl

This is one of the easiest edible containers to grow, making it a great project for kids! Plant an entire slightly shallow container (wider than it is deep) with seeds. Four dollars'-worth of seed will fill 10 pots. When it's too cold out you can bring the container into the garage or to a windowsill. Some suggestions: lettuce, arugula, mizuna, and other cool-weather greens.

Edible Winter Window Boxes

Window boxes dress up the outside of the house, but they're also fun to view from indoors, especially during winter! I like to plant leafy greens in the window box outside my kitchen window. The western sun shines through the foliage of Swiss chard, lettuce and mustard, making them look like they're made of stained glass. They are well suited to be grown with pansies, snapdragons and violas. I also like to add colorful varieties of grass-like carex (sedge) for texture.

Elegant Entryway

Put your front porch pots to work for you during the winter! This is my favorite combination: start with one small or dwarf evergreen shrub as the thriller, add Swiss chard, then stagger seedings of radish so they don't mature all at once and you end up with more than you can eat — followed by bare spots in the pot. Finish with violas for trailing color.

Broccoli Barrel

A lot of gardeners grow broccoli in a barrel even if they have plenty of "in-ground" space so that they can easily replace the soil every year. Cruciferous crops like broccoli are particularly susceptible to soil-borne fungal diseases, so this is a good plan. To make the broccoli barrel more interesting, add come colorful flowers and trailing groundcovers. See page 63 for tips on caring for broccoli.

Fall Feast

What's better than roasted root vegetables seasoned with your own herbs? Here are my favorites: carrots, parsnips and turnips; rosemary, culinary sage and thyme. The sage and thyme in this container group are perennial, so they can stay as you pop other herbs in and out. If you live where rosemary is hardy, a rosemary topiary makes a great center feature plant.

Planting Perfect Pots

It is definitely an old wives' tale that you have to put rocks or pot shards in the bottom of a container for drainage. It's much better to just have good-quality lightweight soil throughout the entire pot.

Fill the containers halfway with soil to start. Then, place the largest plant into the pot and check positioning. The top of the root ball should be 1"-2" below the top edge of the pot. Once you have the larger plants in place you can add more soil. Next, place any other 4" transplants or plugs, checking the depth. The top of the soil ball for these plants should line up with the larger ones. Fill in with soil. Finally, sow seeds according to package instructions and keep them moist while germinating.

Top with ½" of shredded hardwood bark mulch for a tidy appearance and moisture-retention.

Top-dress container plants with a granular organic fertilizer or water in with an organic water-soluble solution, like fish emulsion.

Care & Maintenance

Winter pots require far less care than summer pots because they won't dry out as quickly, but keep an eye on moisture levels. Seeds need to stay moist while germinating, but you don't have to water the entire pot until it is soggy. You'll probably need to water once or twice a week once everything has sprouted. Since cool season plants grow at a much slower rate, they are a lot less needy than warm season plants. I usually top-dress my pots with an organic granular fertilizer upon planting and evaluate fertility needs every 6-8 weeks by applying an organic, nutrient-rich liquid feed like fish emulsion.

In the heat of the summer, your container plants' water needs will require more attention. Self-watering containers are great, especially if you live where it's hot and humid day and night. As the plants grow and their roots take up more space in the pots, you'll have to water more frequently – sometimes twice a day. I try to fertilize my containers once a month with a water-soluble organic fertilizer mixed in a watering can. This provides the essential nutrients to retain healthy foliage while flowering and setting fruit. And remember, these containers are supposed to be pretty, so when a plant starts to look past its prime, pull it out and replace it with something else.

Harvesting

The same harvesting rules apply to these plants as in-ground plants. Check cucumbers, tomatoes and squash daily in the summer and harvest ripe fruits. Peppers and eggplants can go a few days between checks. Trim greens and herbs and pull root vegetables as you need them for meals.

ALTERNATIVE GROWING SYSTEMS
Aeroponics, Aquaponics, Hydroponics

If you haven't heard much about aeroponic, aquaponic and hydroponic growing systems, you soon will. As outdoor spaces shrink and personal schedules become busier, these automated systems are getting a lot of attention. With high yields and increased disease prevention, the three "ponic" systems offer an attractive alternative for the modern-day grower – and you won't even get your hands dirty!

Alternative growing systems, or water-based (soilless) units, are efficient, attractive and easy to manage. Though traditionally utilized in controlled environments, these systems can be incorporated into the landscape. Any location with a half-day of bright sun and access to electricity is an opportunity waiting to happen!

Aeroponic, aquaponic and hydroponic growing offers a unique and engaging experience for people of all ages. Two cases in point: my mechanically inclined husband, who quickly became intrigued, his interest piqued by his love of pumps and electricity, things traditional gardening doesn't offer; and my 10-year-old helper, Aidan, who enjoys mixing and applying the nutrient solutions; he can watch the plants respond and has gained a comprehensive understanding of fertility deficiencies. These systems are important teaching tools to express the chemistry that is required to make a plant grow, thrive and bear fruit.

History

All three growing systems are related and all three are soilless and use water in various ways. Hydroponics, though, is the original system. Its name means "working water," with *hydro* meaning water and *ponos* meaning labor. Water systems like hydroponics have been utilized for thousands of years in diverse civilizations – from ancient Egypt and the Hanging Gardens of Babylon to the floating gardens of the Mexico Aztecs. This ancient method of growing plants remains a practical and innovative approach to cultivating food.

Significant advancements in hydroponic technology have been made over the last century as horticulturists and scientists experimented with different methods of growing. One of the potential applications of hydroponics that drove this research was growing fresh produce in non-arable areas of the world and land with little to no soil. For example, hydroponics were used during World War II to supply food for U.S. troops stationed on islands in the Pacific, and now, even NASA has integrated water systems into the space program.

Today, the ideals surrounding these growing techniques include ending world hunger, reducing food miles, conserving water and supplying the world with safe food to eat. These techniques have become a powerful tool in the classroom, as well, as educators are realizing the diverse applications that water systems can have to teach children about science, gardening, nutrition and more.

The benefits of alternative growing systems

- **Affordability:** Get started with a low budget and use the systems for years.
- **Convenience:** Grow food in any space, inside or out.
- **Water Conservation:** Use up to 2/3 less water than conventional growing.
- **Success:** Produce better tasting, healthier, higher yields with much less input.
- **Year-Round Produce:** Extend the season by easily growing indoors.
- **Family Experience:** Spend quality family time together and teach children the science of how plants grow.

First attempt with Aquaponic growing

How I became a convert. Practical reasons drove me into researching how to utilize water systems in my home landscape. Soil-borne diseases and root knot nematodes, the result of previous decades of farming tobacco in my Southern state, prevented me from growing some of my favorite edibles, namely heirloom tomatoes. These often-unavoidable soil issues can be overcome by moving some or all of your growing out of the ground and into the water.

Select a System

There are a lot of options in the realm of alternative growing systems – and a great number of books and online sites to guide you through choosing which system to try. I'll give you a short primer here and you can continue your research at your leisure.

Your first step will be to identify your goal: what are you trying to grow, how much and where? Spend time researching the available technologies and understand the difference between the three major types of water-based growing.

Aeroponics

Aeroponic kits are becoming hugely popular. Offering easy, space-saving solutions, systems like the Tower Garden® are delivered to your doorstep with everything you will need to succeed. Aeroponics operates with a timer that runs for a period of time (15 minutes) and then shuts off, allowing the air to help "prune" or reduce the overall root mass. Nutrient-rich water is pumped to the top of the unit, allowing gravity to flush the water over the roots of the plants. The results are astounding and these systems can be used year-round as they are mobile and attractive.

Personal note: In my experience, the Tower Garden has been a most effective and user-friendly growing system. This company has a great educational outreach program supporting elementary schools. I have not experimented with other aeroponic systems.

Cherry tomatoes growing in a Tower Garden.

Besides the fish, there many factors that influence an aquaponics system, including the type of food the fish are eating, the size and material of the tank and the seasonal sunlight and temperature. Sunken plastic pond liners in part shade have been the most successful in my home garden, as the insulation from the earth keeps the water cool and the plastic does not release any toxins. Beware of using common animal "feed tanks," as these basins will release zinc which will poison the fish and cause serious nutrient deficiencies in the plants.

Learn from my mistakes! Growing fish in feed tanks leads to zinc toxicity and nutrient deficiencies in the plants.

Aquaponics

Aquaponic systems involve growing fish and plants in harmony by combining aquaculture (raising fish) and hydroponics (the soilless growing of plants). Fish and plants will live happily in one integrated system, or the fish tank water can be pumped to the plants in different containers. The main point is that the fish waste provides an organic food source for the crops and the plants provide a natural filter for the water the fish live in.

Personal note: This approach can be a bit more complicated to set up. It is paramount to research what fish to cultivate, either for pleasure or consumption. I decided to grow the western mosquitofish *(Gambusia affinis)*, a small species of freshwater fish that reproduces rapidly.

This deep water sumbersion Hydroponics system uses only one pump for ten 5 gallons buckets.

Hydroponics

Hydroponic growing is best known and is very accessible in stores and through online resources. There are several different systems that can be purchased depending on the crops and space needed for the setup. The critical component of all hydroponic systems, though: you must have well-aerated, nutrient-rich water flowing to the plants at all times. Sunlight needs vary, depending upon the variety and season. Most importantly, all elements need to be made from a UV-rated plastic to reduce algae growth. I recommend searching hydroponic supply companies online and in person before investing. Start on a small scale, learn the process of growing in water and become addicted, like I did!

Personal note: One of the many advantages of growing in water is the added longevity and vigor of the crops. Heirloom tomatoes are a great example. My in-ground plants survive less than 4 months and yield approximately 10 pounds of fruit each. In contrast, those same varieties grown in a hydroponic system are thriving and produce an average of 25 pounds over a six-month period.

Single container units such as the General Hydroponics PowerGrower are the perfect fit for first-time users. This attractive unit is suitable for the front porch or back patio and successfully grows anything from lettuce and broccoli to heirloom tomatoes.

Beyond the basics

As your interest and confidence develops, consider units that can be expanded to meet your growing needs. Submersion buckets systems, such as the Hydrofarm Root Spa, have been very effective for growing heirloom tomatoes, cucumbers and peppers in my home landscape. I have also had success with a circulating drip system, which supplies 40 lettuce plants year-round in my small greenhouse with 40% shade cloth.

Grow it!

Many food crops are well suited for growth in a water system. I choose plants that are sensitive to soil-borne diseases and root knot nematode infestations since my garden is plagued by both. I have also had success extending cool season vegetables into the summer with water systems; plants such as lettuce and broccoli benefit from a cooler root zone provided by the flowing water. Experiment by growing your favorite edibles, from arugula to zucchini, and remember, the sky is the limit as these technologies become mainstream food growing options.

You can start with traditionally-grown plants and bare-root them using a hose and bucket of water. This approach works well on larger plants like broccoli, cauliflower, heading lettuce or tomatoes.

You can start with seed grown plants and wash the soil off the roots to install in a water based system.

For easy from-seed plants, such as leafy greens, you can simply scatter seed across the top of the soilless media. Germination usually occurs within 5-10 days.

Cool season

- Arugula
- Broccoli
- Cabbage
- Cauliflower
- Lettuce
- Kale
- Spinach

Warm season

- Basil
- Cucumber
- Eggplant
- Pepper
- Tomato

Lettuce growing in the hydroponics method

Care & Maintenance

Caring for an alternative growing system is not difficult but does require daily assessment. It is vital to have the pumps operating to ensure the water is being aerated and that nutrients are flowing (be sure to check outlets following a storm). Adding a nutrient solution and balancing the pH are also critical components for success. Without soil as a buffer, plants will show signs of nutrient deficiency quickly. Over time, you will develop a routine based on the crops and climate conditions you are growing in. For example, in the heat of the Carolina summer, I was adding 3-5 gallons of water each day to the heirloom tomatoes. Every third day, I added 2 gallons of nutrient solution pre-mixed in a watering can to ensure healthy growth and fruit set. As the days shortened and temperatures moderated, this schedule was reduced to once a week. Each type of system will have unique management needs.

Part Three:

YARD TO TABLE

Very soon you will have a yard full of food. How do you get it to the table – or the fridge, freezer and cupboard shelf? Part Three is all about the harvesting, processing, preserving and preparing – including some of my all-time favorite recipes!

Harvesting, Processing & Preserving

THE HARVEST is the most intuitive part of foodscaping. When something looks ripe, I want to pick it! Once you harvest (if you don't eat it on the spot) it's time to process and preserve and enjoy the fantastic edibles you've been growing. Here's how to take your food from the yard to the pantry.

Harvest

If you're new to growing your own, this can be one of the more confusing aspects. When is it ripe? Which part do I harvest?

Sweet corn is ready to eat right when the silks are just turning brown.

One easy way to learn how to harvest which edible is to look at the part of the plant you'll be eating: fruits, leaves & stems, grains & seeds – or the whole plant or roots. The following is not a scientific determination, but more of a guide to getting the most from your plants.

Fruits

Fruits are the reproductive parts of the plants. They are the parts of the plants that have seeds. In the lists below, you'll see a few plants that you might consider "vegetables" but which are actually fruits, botanically speaking. It's helpful to know that bit of botany when you're figuring out how to go about harvesting.

To harvest the fruits, pull or cut them off the plant when they ripen. Here are some tips:

- **Eggplant:** The smaller the better so they're tender and not seedy.

- **Fresh peas and beans:** Harvest when the flower just fades at the end of the pea pod.

- **Melons:** Fruits will be fully-colored. Watermelons will sound a little hollow when you thump them. Softer melons like cantaloupe will actually start to smell like ripe fruit.

- **Peppers:** Harvest before the first fall frost. Pick when plump, shiny and have changed color *(note: some green peppers won't change color)*.

- **Soybeans:** You can pick individual pods when they're slightly smaller than the size of your pinky finger, or you can pull up the whole plant.
- **Summer squash:** The smaller the better!
- **Sweet corn:** When the silks are just starting to turn brown and there's a bit of give in the kernel when you push it with your thumb.
- **Tomatoes:** Pick when the fruits are the expected color (red, yellow, orange, etc.).
- **Winter squash and pumpkins:** Fruits should be fully colored and have a slightly hollow sound when thumped. Do not leave plants outside in a frost.
- **Zucchini:** The smaller the better!

Leaves & Stems

These are the easiest! Snip what you want and leave the rest of the plant to keep growing. Cut off the flowers of basil when they appear so the plants put energy into growing more of their fragrant leaves. For lettuce, spinach, other greens and

Cut kohlrabi off just below its bulbous bottom. The leaves are edible too, steamed or fresh!

cilantro, however, the harvest cannot be prolonged by cutting off the flowers. All of these plants are edible at every stage of their growing cycle:

- Arugula
- Basil
- Celery
- Cilantro
- Dill
- Kale
- Kohlrabi
- Lettuce & Salad Greens
- Mustard
- Oregano
- Parsley
- Rosemary
- Sage
- Spinach
- Swiss Chard
- Thyme

Young lettuce and mustard greens

Potatoes are ready to harvest when the foliage turns brown.

Whole Plant or Root Vegetables

You'll remove the entire plant when harvesting these vegetables, with a few notable exceptions.

- **Beets:** Harvest as needed when the top of the root develops into a globe 2-5" wide.
- **Broccoli:** When heads are fully formed, and the green florets are still tight.
- **Cabbage:** The head should still be tight when you harvest. Check seed packet for days to maturity.
- **Carrots:** Harvest throughout the season, starting when the top of the root is the width of your thumbnail.
- **Cauliflower:** Heads are well developed but still tight.

Pull up peanuts and let them bake in the sun to dry out (you can let the entire plants bake or separate peanuts from the plants). Bring them inside, shell them and roast them.

Carrots are a favorite root crop.

- **Pak choi (or bok choy):** Harvest as you are ready to use.
- **Peanuts:** The leaves will turn yellow, indicating it is time to harvest. Pull out of ground and allow to dry in the sun for several days before processing.
- **Potatoes:** Foliage will start to turn brown. For new potatoes, dig when foliage is at least 12" tall.
- **Rutabagas:** Harvest when roots are 3-5" in size.
- **Sweet Potatoes:** Harvest when you're ready to change the bed to install cool-weather crops. Size will vary.
- **Turnips:** Any time for greens. Check plants and harvest when roots are 3" in diameter. They're oversized (and will be woody) when they're larger than your fist.

Wheat, mid-harvest.

Grains & Seeds

Let the whole plant dry in the landscape before you harvest. Cut or pull up the entire plant and let it hang-dry over a clean sheet or newspaper to collect seed. Some plants, such as sesame, will naturally release seed. Other plants have to be threshed and winnowed, which is the act of removing seed from the pods or flower heads and separating it from chaff (the rest of the plant material). Rice is heat-threshed, while oats and wheat have to be threshed by beating the grain stalks over a bucket and then winnowed to remove chaff.

- Barley
- Buckwheat
- Corn
- Dry Peas and Beans
- Oats
- Rice
- Sesame
- Sunflower
- Wheat

Processing & Preserving

Processing and preserving go hand-in-hand. Processing is about the way you prepare the food for preserving (saving it for later). The way you do both depends on how much time you have, how much space you have for different types of storage, and what makes up the bulk of your daily diet. I am a huge fan of using time in the most efficient way possible, and I have equal freezer and pantry space, so I will often can some and freeze some; I can't just do one or the other. I also try to choose the method that most efficiently utilizes the food.

Freeze

You can wash, dry thoroughly and freeze these edibles in freezer bags:

- Basil
- Blueberries
- Cilantro
- Ground Corn
- Oats
- Raspberries
- Wheat

Blanch & Freeze

Bring a pot of water to boil and prepare an ice water bath. Boil the vegetables for 30 seconds, then blanch them by plunging them immediately into the ice water bath. Blanching improves the structural quality of the fruits and vegetables and helps preserve the texture of the food.

- Broccoli
- Cauliflower
- Corn
- Onions
- Peppers
- Whole Tomatoes
- Sliced Cabbage
- Soybeans
- Spinach
- Swiss Chard

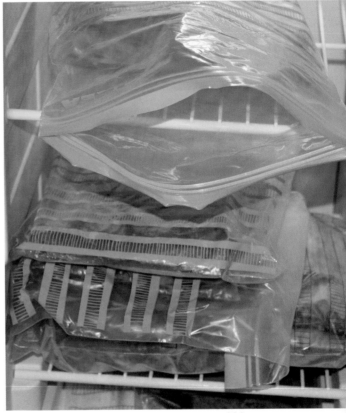

My whole freezer is full of homegrown edibles.

Store Dry

Store potatoes in brown paper bags in a closet that has space. Since most modern houses don't have root cellars, there's no shame in storing food in a bedroom closet. Just warn guests in advance!

- Beans
- Garlic
- Lentils
- Onions
- Oregano
- Peanuts
- Peas
- Potato
- Rosemary
- Sage
- Sweet Potato
- Thyme

A pan of roasted vegetables waiting to become something yummy!

Roast & Freeze

These can be roasted separately and frozen, or in groups to use as a basis for soups or sauces, etc. See page 168 for a delicious tomato sauce recipe. You can roast onions and garlic and freeze together as a paste for cooking.

- Eggplant
- Garlic
- Onions
- Pepper
- Tomato

I store some of my potato crop in the closet – a real space saver.

Canned homemade tomato juice.

Can

I don't can-preserve all of my harvests because it is time- and labor-intensive and takes up a lot of pantry space that I do not have. Over the years I have figured what is best for me to freeze (like tomato paste) and which harvests deserve to be canned. I have narrowed it down to two favorites: candied peppers and tomato juice. You will find these instructions in the Recipes section.

I now combine the canning process for these to maximize my time and energy and am able to preserve more than 50 quarts in a few hours. The trick is planning in advance and having a well-timed strategy. Through the summer I freeze the tomato juice as I am processing and roasting paste. As the water in the stovetop canner is warming to a boil, I heat the tomato juice, then fill jars and load the canner. While that is boiling for the necessary 15 minutes, I slice the peppers and begin the candying process. This strategy helps me make the most of the boiling hot water in the canner while I preserve my favorite flavors from the foodscape.

Refrigerate

Is there anything better than freshly harvested produce? Even if you are growing a small foodscape with only a few types of edibles, having access to these fresh ingredients will enhance every meal. If processing, canning and freezing are too big a task, simply store your harvest in the refrigerator and eat some daily. Here is a super tip for prolonging the freshness of green produce: put the cut ends into a glass or jar of water and cover with a bag or plastic wrap. It will last a LOT longer than stashing it in a bag in a drawer to rot.

- Asparagus
- Broccoli, Cauliflower, and other brassicas
- Carrot
- Corn
- Cucumber
- Kale & Collards
- Lettuce and Salad Greens
- Melon
- Spinach
- Squash
- Tomato (once sliced; otherwise, tomatoes will last longer when stored at room temperature)
- Zucchini

Refrigerator pickles are simple to make. Stuff jars with sliced cucumbers, onions, garlic, herbs and peppers and fill with white vinegar. Delicious!

Sharing the Bounty

One of the best parts of growing such a huge harvest is getting to share. A basket of fresh heirloom tomatoes or a jar of pickles or candied peppers is much more meaningful than a store-bought trinket.

A bundle of wheat, a bag of peanuts, a jar of tomato juice — these are all meaningful things you can share with friends and family.

RECIPES

THIS FINAL CHAPTER is a selection of simple, delicious recipes – most of them involving tomatoes because that's what I always have an over-abundance of!

What to do with ALL of those Tomatoes!

Over the years I have found tricks to save time when cooking from scratch. Through many experiments, these tomato recipes have saved me countless hours and allowed me to make as much or as little as desired.

Random tomato thoughts

- I always juice my tomatoes to reduce the amount of liquid that has to cook off. This is a simple process of squeezing the raw tomato paste between two fine strainers and collecting the juice in a bowl.

- The juice extracted from the raw tomatoes is a delicious base for Bloody Marys.

- The roasted paste can be transformed into tomato soup, marinara sauce, ketchup, salsa — basically anything that requires cooked tomatoes. There are many ways to make delicious tomato sauce. Remember, 94% of a tomato's weight is water, so by separating the juice from the pulp you will reduce the cooking time for roasting by a significant margin.

Heirloom Tomato Juice

Juicing your tomatoes raw is a great way to speed the cooking process up and have a foodscape-fresh beverage to serve guests. I like to sort my heirloom tomatoes by color or variety to make brightly-colored juice of orange, yellow, red and purple. The juice is refreshing served over ice in a ball jar and lid (for regular shaking).

You can also freeze the juice for future parties or preserve it through the canning process to share as party favors and holiday gifts (read on).

Canning

If you have never canned before, tomato juice is a good place to start, as it is simple and fast . This is one thing I take the time to preserve because I do not have enough freezer space to store it all and enjoy sending the "taste of summer" to friends and family as a Winter Solstice gift. For specific canning instructions, consult a canning manual. Instructions will differ for pressure canners and stove stop "water bath" devices. I follow the instructions for tomato juice from the Ball Complete Book of Home Preserving, which involves a 15-minute water bath to preserve the heirloom juice.

Ingredients
8-10 vine-ripened tomatoes, or as many tomatoes as you have

Salt

Brown sugar, honey or sorghum syrup, to taste

Preparation

1. Slice garden fresh tomatoes in quarters and add to food processor

2. Add 1 tablespoon fine salt and brown sugar, honey or sorghum syrup, to taste

3. Pulse for 10-15 seconds

4. Pour through strainer, collecting juice in bowl

5. Squeeze the tomato paste dry (see Practical Heirloom Tomato Paste below for instructions)

6. You can then roast the tomato paste before freezing and proceed to can your tomato juice.

Brie's Homegrown Bloody Mary

Bloody Marys have become a staple for our annual Tomato Tasting Fundraiser. I like to set up a make-your-own station so guests can enjoy a custom drink. Serve in a Mason jar over ice with a lid for regular shaking.

Ingredients

1/2 quart fresh tomato juice

1 tablespoon dill pickle juice

1 tablespoon grated fresh horseradish

1 tablespoon Worcester sauce

1 tablespoon hot sauce

1 tablespoon aged balsamic vinegar

Dash of freshly ground pepper

1 shot of vodka or gin for added spirit

An olive, jalapeno, lime or wedge of cheese for garnish

Preparation

1. Fill a quart jar with tomato juice.

2. Add dill pickle juice, Worchester sauce, hot sauce, horseradish and balsamic vinegar, to taste.

3. Add a shot of vodka or gin.

4. Screw on lid and shake. Keep lid for regular stirring.

Practical Heirloom Tomato Paste

Tomato paste is the base of all things made from cooked tomatoes. Once you have separated the juice from the raw tomatoes, you can simply roast that paste for 45 minutes in a 400°F oven. Once this is cooked, you can freeze it in quart bags for future use or add ingredients to make traditional sauces, salsa, or soup, which can be frozen or canned for cupboard storage, depending on how much time you have.

Ingredients

Raw tomato paste

1 tablespoon salt

1 tablespoon cane or brown sugar

1 garlic bulb, peeled

Preparation

1. Pre-heat over to 400°F.
2. Add tomato paste to roasting pan.
3. Evenly sprinkle salt and sugar on top.
4. Toss in peeled garlic and stir.
5. Roast for 45-60 minutes until paste is bubbling.
6. Cool to room temperature.
7. A. Freeze as roasted paste by adding servings to quart bags and laying flat so that, once they're frozen, you can stand them on end. (You can also keep them flat, but starting flat to freeze ensures they aren't lumpy or misshapen in the freezer.) Or…
7. B. Follow instructions below to make finished sauce, salsa or soup.

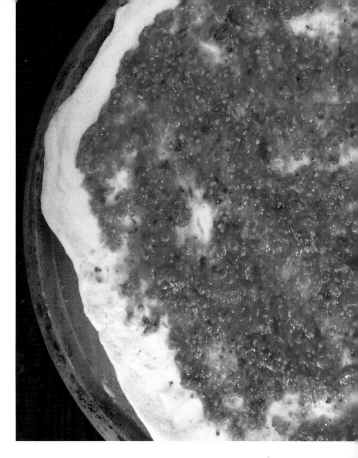

Pizza Sauce

Growing the ingredients for pizza sauce is colorful and easy – plus, it is a great way to engage kids in the yard-to-table movement.

Ingredients

Roasted tomato paste

6 garlic cloves

2 tablespoons olive oil

1 tablespoon salt

1 tablespoon black pepper

1 tablespoon fresh oregano leaves

3 tablespoons fresh basil leaves

1 tablespoon fresh thyme

1 teaspoon crushed red pepper flakes

Preparation

1. In a saucepan, combine ingredients and heat to a simmer.
2. Using an immersion blender, mix the contents into a thick paste.
3. Add 2-3 tablespoons of water, if needed.
4. Remove from heat.
5. Use hot on a home-cooked pizza.
6. Freeze in quart bags or in pressure can for cupboard storage.

Spaghetti Sauce

This is my favorite go-to option for making a delicious "handcrafted meal" when time is tight. This versatile sauce recipe can be used for lasagna or baked penne – basically any dish involving tomato sauce and noodles. I do not find spaghetti to be the most practical of the pasta options; if you and your family prefer elbows, bowties or penne please substitute.

Note: Adding a crumbled bacon topper is a great way to give this meal the "wow" factor. I like to crumble baked bits, which are cooked at 350°F for 20 minutes, or until crisp. Pat slices dry with paper towel and hand crumble. Sprinkle on top for an extra flavor boost.

Ingredients

1 quart bag roasted tomato paste (recipe on page 166)
1 cup water
4 garlic cloves, minced
4 teaspoons dried oregano leaves
4 teaspoons dried basil leaves
1 box pasta (1 lb.)
2 tablespoons olive oil for the pasta water
Salt (to taste for the sauce and to flavor the pasta water)
Freshly grated pepper and Parmesan cheese for garnish

Preparation

1. In a saucepan, combine tomato paste, minced garlic, dried herbs and water.
2. Heat to a low boil, reduce heat to a simmer.
3. Using an immersion blender, mix the contents into a thick paste, reduce heat and cover until pasta is ready.
4. Bring a pot of water to a boil.
5. Add pasta, olive oil and salt, and cook per instructions on box.
6. Taste sauce and adjust seasonings as needed. Remove from heat.
7. Drain and rinse pasta and add to serving bowls.
8. Ladle generous portion of sauce on top of each bowl.
9. Top with freshly grated pepper and Parmesan cheese.

Candied Jalapeño Peppers

This is by far the very best way to preserve that abundant fall harvest of peppers and make everyone you know happy! Candied peppers may sound odd, but they are a delicious treat for nearly any meal and are an ideal holiday gift. They are simple to make and can be done in under an hour. If you are in a time bind, add the washed, stemless peppers to a food processor. Chop into a relish texture and follow the instructions below.

Always wear gloves when handling peppers. I made this mistake several years ago and suffered sore fingertips from exposure to hot pepper seed. Any pepper variety can be candied, not just jalapeños. If you have family members with sensitivity to heat, try candying bell pepper slices — they are delicious! I grow approximately 75-100 mild-flavored pepper plants each season and candy all of my late harvests, resulting in 25-40 quarts of candied peppers from 3 evening sessions of cooking and canning.

I frequently serve these paired with cheese and crackers and use them as a salad topping. They are a favorite sprinkled on top of a plate of nachos. They add a perfect sweet and tangy flavor to pasta dishes and are a great condiment for a sandwich or quesadilla. Basically, these sweet treats complement any dish. Makes 12 quarts.

Ingredients

3 pounds fresh jalapeño peppers

2 cups apple cider vinegar*

6 cups sugar**

1 tablespoon chopped fresh turmeric

10-15 cloves of chopped fresh garlic (depending on how much garlic you like)

* Vinegar type can be substituted based on your preference. I have experimented with many different vinegars, including champagne, rice, white and apple cider. The finished flavors are only slightly different. My go-to is apple cider vinegar because I can buy it in larger quantities at a reasonable price.

** Sugar is a critical ingredient in making candied peppers, as the sweetness cuts the spice, making these palatable for even those intolerant of heat. I have used every kind of sugar I can find: organic cane sugar, sorghum syrup, brown sugar, white granulated sugar. All will do the job, provided you use the right amount – which will seem like way too much, but it isn't!

Instructions

1. Wearing gloves, remove the stems and slice the peppers into uniform $\frac{1}{8}$-$\frac{1}{4}$" rounds.

2. In a large pot, bring vinegar, sugar, turmeric and garlic to a boil. Reduce heat and simmer for 5 minutes.

3. Add the pepper slices and simmer for exactly 4 minutes.

4. Use a slotted spoon to transfer the peppers into clean, sterile, 1-quart canning jars to within $\frac{1}{4}$" of the upper rim of the jar.

5. Ladle syrup into the jars over the jalapeno slices, eliminating air pockets.

6. Wipe the rims of the jars with a clean cloth and cover with new, 2-piece lids, sealed to finger-tip tightness.

To Can: This is the way I can, using a simple stove-top water bath canner.

Note: If you do not want to can these to the point of shelf-stable, you can put the jars in your refrigerator and store them for up to 3 months. However, these are quick and easy to can and I prefer to keep my refrigerator space open.

1. Place jars in a stovetop "water bath" canner and cover with 2" of water.

2. Bring the water to boil. When it reaches a full rolling boil, set the timer for 15 minutes for quarts.

3. When timer rings, turn off heat and use canning tongs to transfer the jars to a cooling rack.

4. Once cooled, label and store in pantry for up to a year.

5. Once opened keep refrigerated.

6. Share with your family and friends!

A Few Last Words

Thank you your interest in foodscaping! It is my sincere hope that you will be inspired by The Foodscape Revolution to see the opportunities that every landscape offers. The possibilities are endless when you embrace the hobby and lifestyle of cultivating a nourishing, beautiful landscape.

When I began my first foodscape it was out of necessity. I wanted to eat quality, organic produce but couldn't afford it. I was fortunate to be able to apply my horticultural know-how to help solve this problem and overcome the tight HOA restrictions that I, and so many of us, live under. It has been my dream to share this knowledge, because accessing healthy food shouldn't be out of reach for all of us who live on tight budgets. I also believe that taking an active interest in growing plants is something that more people need to learn about. It is an enriching activity that works your mind, body and soul. This passion and determination to "make the world a better place" has led me to write this book and share my insights to encourage you to make the most of the landscape you already have.

Foodscaping isn't about living off the grid and it's not about turning all landscapes into farms. This design strategy isn't even new! Long before box stores and highly scrutinized developments, people grew the plants they loved to eat alongside trees, shrubs and flowers. Only in recent times have we endured the concept that food crops must be grown in wooden boxes and that edibles and

flowers can't mingle happily in the landscape. That is a silly notion that should be forgotten!

Next time you are tending your landscape, ask yourself, "Why can't I have it all?" Then consider the possibilities that a foodscape offers: beautiful collection of plants, abundant flowers, a healthy ecosystem – and fresh produce! The logical integration of edibles in traditional landscapes makes too much sense to ignore. It is a design strategy aimed to make even the smallest patches of ground bountiful.

This is a land management practice that relies on organic growing techniques that are safe for you, your family and pets. Traditional maintenance practices like mulching and edging keep the space looking clean and tidy. But, unlike the common landscapes that surround us, foodscapes are meant to be living ecosystems that meet aesthetic needs while serving a greater purpose for the environment and kitchen. Flowering ornamental plants offer biodiversity which will increase populations of beneficial pollinators and wildlife. Seasonal edibles provide dynamic color and texture while making it easy to gather fresh food for every meal. And for the neighbor and passerby who sees what's growing in your yard (that ripe tomato hanging within a blooming hydrangea, those peppers woven within the pink muhly grass, the sweeping mass of amber waves of grain), you're raising awareness of how and where food grows and where food belongs. That's the message of foodscaping.

I encourage you to utilize the resources that you have access to: a sunny foundation landscape, a boring property border, a school campus, or a neighborhood entry. All of these common landscapes represent an opportunity to grow nutritious produce while cultivating a beautiful space. The sun, soil and irrigation systems are just waiting to be harnessed for the greater good of health, wellness, community and the environment.

Growing food has empowered me to set my hopes high and envision a future where landscapes provide more. I hope it will do the same for you. So, dream big and join the revolution by making the most of the land you already manage. Share your journey through The Foodscape Revolution Facebook page and participate in the movement that will transform how local food is cultivated.

Happy foodscaping!
Brie

Brie Arthur Links:

https://BrieGrows.com

www.BrieGrows.com

Find me on Facebook:
The Foodscape Revolution; Brie Grows

Follow the Revolution on Instagram:
@BrieThePlantLady

and on Twitter:
@FoodscapeRev

Articles about Foodscaping:

- The Foodscaping Mission: http://magazine.ornamentalbreeder.com/article/may-2016/cover-story-think-outside-the-raised-box.aspx

- Foodscaping the Suburbs: httph://vimeo.com/101100044

- OG: http://www.organicgardening.com/living/the-new-generation?page=0,1

- Bullock Garden: https://m.youtube.com/watch?feature=youtu.be&v=B5aEIdCWOQE

- GGWTV: http://www.growingagreenerworld.com/making-more-plants

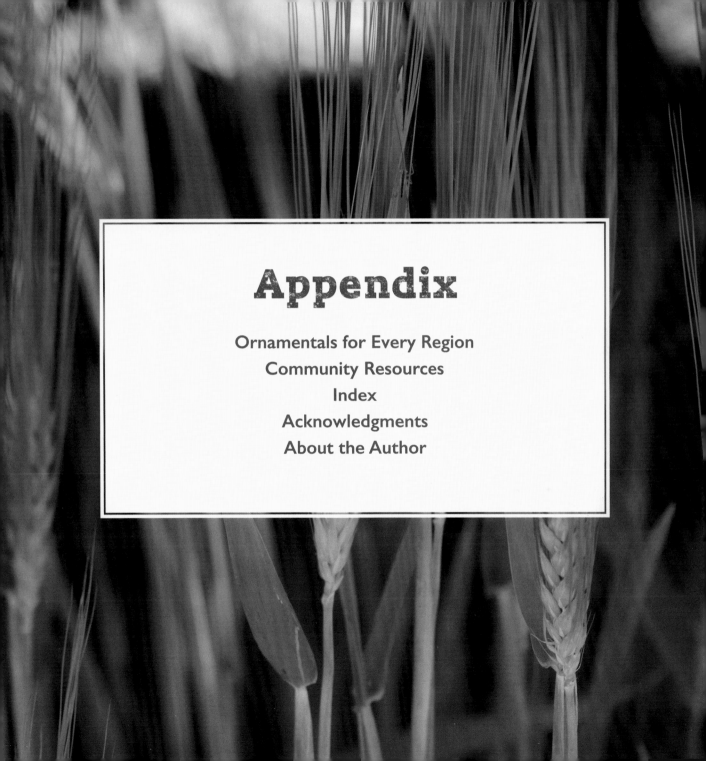

Appendix

Ornamentals for Every Region
Community Resources
Index
Acknowledgments
About the Author

ORNAMENTALS FOR EVERY REGION
Plant selections to enhance your foodscape framework

Even if you're starting with a reasonably complete ornamental landscape, you might want to enhance the biodiversity or add multi-season interest. Of course, the ideal plant palette for Ohio is going to be different from one for Florida or California or Maine. Which is why I've asked some of the best horticulturists from 15 different regions to weigh in with their top ornamental plant picks for your foodscape framework. Though they chose different numbers and types of assortments – some more extensive than others – what these contributors have in common is decades'-worth of gardening experience, so you can be confident that you'll be successful when growing their recommended plants. My thanks to these contributors for sending us their favorites.

Northeast
Angela Treadwell-Palmer
Plant Marketing, Plants Nouveau, LLC

Elephant Ear, *Colocasia* 'Painted Black Gecko'

Ninebark, *Physocarpus opulifolius* 'Diabolo'

Panicle Hydrangea, *Hydrangea paniculata* 'Bokraflame' Magical® Fire Candle

Rose, *Rosa* 'Zephirine Drouhin'

Weigela, *Weigela* 'Kolmagira' Rainbow Sensation™

Mid-Atlantic
Janet Draper
Horticulturist, Smithsonian Institution

Adam's Needle Yucca, *Yucca filamentosa*

Beaked Yucca, *Yucca rostrata*

Blue Shadow Fothergilla, *Fothergilla* × *intermedia* 'Blue Shadow'

Boxwood, *Buxus* spp.

DeGroot's Spire Arborvitea, *Thuja* 'DeGroot's Spire'

Fastigiate False Yew, *Cephalotaxus* 'Fastigiata'

Flushing Yew, *Taxus* 'Flushing'

Globosa Nana Japanese Cedar, *Cryptomeria japonica* 'Globosa Nana'

Kosteri False Cypress, *Chamaecyparis obtusa* 'Kosteri'

Limelight Panicle Hydrangea, *Hydrangea paniculata* 'Limelight'

Montgomery Spruce, *Picea* 'Montgomery'

Oakleaf Hydrangea, *Hydrangea quercifolia*

Palibin Lilac, *Syringa meyeri* 'Palibin'

Tanyosho Pine, *Pinus densiflora* 'Umbraculifera'

Mid-Atlantic
Barbara Katz
Landscape Designer, London Landscapes, LLC

Autumn Charm Upright Sedum, *Sedum* Autumn Charm™

Blue Boa Anise Hyssop, *Agastache* 'Blue Boa'

Blue Paradise Upright Phlox, *Phlox paniculata* 'Blue Paradise'

Catlin's Giant Bugleweed, *Ajuga reptans* 'Catlin's Giant'

Cherry Dazzle Crape Myrtle, *Lagerstroemia* Cherry Dazzle®

Chocolate Chip Bugleweed, *Ajuga* 'Chocolate Chip'

Common Laurel, *Prunus laurocerasus* 'Mount Vernon'

Cosmic Eye Tickseed, *Coreopsis* 'Cosmic Eye'

Five Colored Holly Osmanthus, *Osmanthus heterophyllus* 'Goshiki'

Glow Girl Spiraea, *Spiraea betulifolia* 'Glow Girl'

Golden Jubilee Anise Hyssop, *Agastache* 'Golden Jubilee'

Jeana Upright Phlox, *Phlox paniculata* 'Jeana'

Little Lime Panicle Hydrangea, *Hydrangea paniculata* 'Jane'

Mel's Blue Stoke's Aster, *Stokesia laevis* 'Mel's Blue'

Nidiformis Norway Spruce, *Picea abies* 'Nidiformis'

Poet's Laurel, *Danae racemosa*

Red Sentinel Astilbe, *Astilbe* 'Red Sentinel'

Rozanne Geranium, *Geranium* 'Rozanne'

Sagae Hosta, *Hosta* 'Sagae'

Southeast
Preston Montague
Landscape Designer

Fall Blooming Camellia, *Camellia sasanqua*

Oakleaf Hydrangea, *Hydrangea quercifolia*

Panicle Hydrangea, *Hydrangea paniculata*

Pink Azalea, *Rhododendron periclymenoides*

Ruby Spice Summersweet, *Clethra alnifolia* 'Ruby Spice'

Sixteen Candles Summersweet, *Clethra alnifolia* 'Sixteen Candles'

Southeast
Jenks Farmer
Designer, Jenks Farmer Plantsman

Chinese Quince, *Pseudocydonia sinensis*

Fuyu Persimmon, *Diospyros* 'Fuyu'

Hopi and Podsednik Pecan, *Carya illinoiensis* 'Hopi' and 'Podsednik'

Keiffer Pear, *Pyrus communis* 'Kieffer'

Nesbit Muscadine Grape, *Vitus rotundifolia* 'Nesbit'

Owari Satsuma Mandarin Orange, *Citrus reticulata* 'Owari'

Paw Paw, *Asimina triloba*

Pineapple Guava, *Acca sellowiana*

Pomegranate, *Punica granatum*

Deep South
Bobby Green
Green Nurseries and Landscape

Alabama Azalea, *Rhododendron alabamense*

Bigleaf Hydrangea, *Hydrangea macrophylla*

Blueberries, *Vaccinium*

Dancing Ladies Ginger, *Globba winittii*

Fall Bloooming Camellia, *Camellia sasanqua*

Fragrant Tea Olive, *Osmanthus fragrans* 'Fodzinghu'

Ginger Lily, *Hedychium coronarium*

Hidden Cone Ginger, *Curcuma cordata*

Kumquat, *Fortunella japonica*

Meyer Lemon, *Citrus* × *meyeri*

Owari Satsuma Mandarin Orange, *Citrus reticulata* 'Owari'

Piedmont Azalea, *Rhododedron canescens*

Swamp Azalea, *Rhododendron viscosum*

Tea Camellia, *Camellia sinensis*

Vernal Camellia, *Camellia* × *vernalis*

Winter Blooming Camellia, *Camellia japonica*

Florida
Teresa Watkins
Landscape Designer,
Sustainable Horticultural Environments

Abutilon, *Abutilon* × *hybridum*

African Iris, *Dietes vegeta*

Encore® Azaleas, *Rhododendron* spp.

Firebush, *Hamelia patens*

Giant Apostles Iris, *Neomarica caerulea* 'Regina'

Muhly Grass, *Muhlenbergia capillaris*

Panama Rose, *Rondeletia splendens*

Pinwheel Jasmine, *Tabernaemontana divaricata*

Plumbago, *Plumbago auriculata*

Princess Flower, *Tibouchina* spp.

Simpson's Stopper, or Twinberry, *Myrcianthes fragrans*

Great Lakes
Maria Zampini
President, UpShoot LLC

American Cranberry Bush, *Viburnum trilobum*

Black Tower Elderberry, *Sambucus nigra* 'Black Tower'

Blueberry, *Vaccinium* spp.

Bright Lights Swiss Chard, *Beta vulgaris* 'Bright Lights'

Bonfire Ornamental Peach, *Prunus persica* 'Bonfire'

Cinderella Crabapple, *Malus* spp.

Cornelian Cherry, *Cornus mas*

Currant, *Ribes rubrum*

Dwarf Serviceberry, *Amelanchier arborea* 'Autumn Brilliance' and 'Spring Glory'

Eastern Redbud, *Cercis canadensis*

Gooseberry, *Ribes uva-crispa*

Hardy Kiwi, *Actinidia arguta*

Hazelnut, *Corylus avellana*

Lancelot Crabapple, *Malus* spp.

Lollipop Crabapple, *Malus* spp.

Natal Plum, *Carissa*

Ornamental Rhubarb, *Rheum palmatum* 'Tanguticum'

Upper Mid-West
Christa Steenwyk
Creative Director, Walters Gardens, Inc.

Black Pearl Coral Bells, Heuchera PRIMO™ 'Black Pearl'

Cat's Meow Catmint, *Nepeta* 'Cat's Meow'

Daisy May Shasta Daisy, *Leucanthemum superbum* Daisy May®

Going Bananas Daylily, *Hemerocallis* 'Going Bananas'

Grape Expectations Coral Bells, *Heuchera* 'Grape Expectations'

Millenium Ornamental Onion *Allium* 'Millenium'

Opening Act Upright Phlox, *Phlox* 'Opening Act White'

Pardon My Cerise Bee Balm, *Monarda* 'Pardon My Cerise'

Prince Charming Butterfly Bush, Buddleia MONARCH® 'Prince Charming'

Salsa Red Coneflower, Echinacea SOMBRERO® Salsa Red

Zinfin Doll Hydrangea, *Hydrangea paniculata* Zinfin Doll™

Central Mid-West
Kelly D. Norris
Director of Horticulture,
Greater Des Moines Botanical Garden

Big Bluestem, *Andropogon gerardii* 'Red October'

Black-Eyed Susan, *Rudbeckia subtomentosa* 'Henry Eilers'

Bush Honeysuckle, *Diervilla* 'Kodiak Orange' and 'Kodiak Black'

Carefree Beauty Rose, *Rosa* 'Carefree Beauty'

False Goat's Beard, *Sorbaria sorbifolia* 'Sem'

Fountain Grass, *Pennisetum alopecuroides* 'Ginger Love'

Golden Clematis, *Clematis tangutica* 'Helios'

Issai Beautyberry, *Callicarpa dichotoma* 'Issai'

Little Lime® Panicle Hydrangea, *Hydrangea paniculata* 'Jane'

Smooth Hydrangea, *Hydrangea arborescens* 'Haas Halo'

Witherod Viburnum, Viburnum cassinoides 'Freedom'

Lower Midwest
Caleb Melchior
Landscape Designer

American Hazelnut, *Corylus americana*

Buttercup Winterhazel, *Corylopsis pauciflora*

Chinese Chestnut, *Castanea mollissima*

Chinese Witch Hazel, *Hamamelis mollis*

Common Hazelnut, *Corylus avellana*

Crabapple, *Malus* spp.

Dwarf Fothergilla, *Fothergilla gardenii*

Dwarf Sweetspire, *Itea virginica* 'Little Henry'

Elderberry, *Sambucus nigra*

Hardy Sweet Box, *Sarcococca hookeriana* var. *humilis*

Japanese Boxwood, *Buxus microphylla* var. *japonica*

Korean Spice Viburnum, *Viburnum* × *carlesii*

Oakleaf Hydrangea, *Hydrangea quercifolia*

Paw Paw, *Asimina triloba*

Persimmon, *Diospyrus virginiana*

Summersweet Clethra, *Clethra alnifolia*

Serviceberry, *Amelanchier canadensis*

East Texas
Jared Barnes
Assistant Professor of Horticulture, SFA State University

Blueberry, *Vaccinium ashei* 'Tifblue' and 'O'Neal'

Flame Azalea, *Rhododendron austrinum*

Flame Willow, *Salix* 'Flame'

Golden Possumhaw, *Ilex decidua* 'Finch's Golden'

Jelena Witch Hazel, *Hamamelis* 'Jelena'

Magnolia, *Magnolia platypetala*

Orange Storm Flowering Quince, *Chaenomeles* 'Orange Storm'

Pineapple Guava, *Acca sellowiana*

Snowflake Oakleaf Hydrangea, *Hydrangea quercifolia* 'Snowflake'

Tea Camellia, *Camellia sinensis*

Whiteleaf Mountain Mint, *Pycnanthemum albescens*

Wintersweet, *Chimonanthus praecox*

Yellow Flowered Hibiscus, *Hibiscus hamabo*

Central Texas
Leslie Finical Halleck
Halleck Horticultural, LLC

Autumn Sage, *Salvia greggii*

Barometerbush, *Leucophyllum langmaniae* 'Lynn's Legacy'

Barometerbush, *Leucophyllum langmaniae* 'Rio Bravo'

Dwarf Abelia, *Abelia* 'Kaleidoscope'

Dwarf Abelia, *Abelia* 'Mardi Gras'

Dwarf Abelia, *Abelia* 'Rose Creek'

Laurustinus, *Viburnum tinus* 'Spring Bouquet'

Rosemary, *Rosmarinus officinalis*

White Mistflower, *Eupatorium wrightii*

Wonderful Pomegranate, *Punica granatum* 'Wonderful'

Lower Plains
Todd Lasseigne
President, Tulsa Botanic Garden

Autumn Sage, *Salvia greggii*

Bird of Paradise Shrub, *Caesalpinia gilliesii*

Butcher's Broom, *Ruscus aculeatus*

Dwarf Abelia, *Abelia* 'Radiance'

Dwarf Oakleaf Hydrangea, *Hydrangea quercifolia* 'Munchkin'

Evergreen Candytuft, *Iberis sempervirens*

False Lilac, *Leptodermis oblonga*

Fragrant Sumac, *Rhus aromatica*

Golden Spiraea, *Spiraea thunbergii* 'Ogon'

Korean Spice Viburnum, *Viburnum carlesii*

Little Lime® Panicle Hydrangea, *Hydrangea paniculata* 'Jane'

Mock Orange, *Philadelphus* 'Belle Etoile'

Mongolian Gold Clematis, *Clematis fruticosa* 'Mongolian Gold'

Persian Lilac, *Syringa* × *persica*

Pink Indigo, *Indigofera amblyantha*

Possumhaw Viburnum, *Viburnum nudum*

Sunburst St. John's Wort, *Hypericum frondosum* 'Sunburst'

Taylor's Rudolph Dwarf Yaupon Holly, *Ilex vomitoria* 'Taylor's Rudolph'

Variegated Five-leafed Aralia, *Eleutherococcus sieboldianus* 'Variegatus'

Virginia Sweetspire, *Itea virginica*

Rocky Mountains
Panayoti Kelaidis
Senior Curator and Director of Outreach
Denver Botanic Gardens

Boxwood, *Buxus sempervirens* 'Vardar Valley' and 'Green Mountain'

Creeping Cotoneaster, *Cotoneaster apiculatus* 'Tom Thumb'

Dwarf Burning Bush, *Euonymus alatus* 'Compacta'

Manchurian Viburnum, *Viburnum burejaeticum* 'PO17S'

Tom Thumb Arborvitae, *Thuja occidentalis* 'Tom Thumb'

White Spruce, *Picea glauca* 'Albertina'

Winnipeg Parks Rose, *Rosa* 'Winnipeg Parks'

Pacific Northwest
Rizaniño Reyes
Plant Introductions & Garden Design

Blueberry, *Vaccinium* 'Sunshine Blue'

Box Honeysuckle, *Lonicera nitida* 'Twiggy'

Cavatine Japanese Andromeda, *Pieris japonica* 'Cavatine'

Fall Blooming Camellia, *Camellia sasanqua*

Fortune's Osmanthus, *Osmanthus* x *fortunei*

Mountain Laurel, *Kalmia latifolia*

Portland Rose, *Rosa* 'Rose de Rescht'

Red Flowering Currant, *Ribes sanguineum*

Red Osier Dogwood, *Cornus sericea*

Rosemary, *Rosmarinus officinalis*

Ruby Slippers Oakleaf Hydrangea, *Hydrangea quercifolia* 'Ruby Slippers'

Strawberry Tree, *Arbutus unedo* 'Compacta'

Southern California
Wendy Shinar
Horticulturist

Bird of Paradise, *Strelitzia reginae*

Calla Lily, *Zantedeschia aethiopica*

Citrus Trees, *Citrus* spp.
　　Full-Size: Lemon, Lime, Nectarine, Orange
　　Dwarf: Kumquat, Lime, Mandarin Orange, Orange

Grapes, *Vitus*

Kangaroo Paws, *Anigozanthos*

Lemongrass, *Cymbopogon citratus*

Loquat, *Eriobotrya japonica*

Milkweed, *Asclepias*

New Zealand Flax, *Phormium*

Passion Fruit, *Passiflora edulis*

Pink Breath of Heaven, *Coleonema pulchrum*

Plum, *Prunus* spp.

Winter Blooming Camellia, *Camellia japonica*

THE FOODSCAPE REVOLUTION:
Community Resources

Taking the Foodscape Revolution beyond your landscape is an important way to influence the community you live in. There are a lot of different strategies to connect with the people living in your neighborhood, town and beyond. I recommend starting simple and building momentum one season at a time.

Join an organization

The American Horticultural Society is a great place to get started. One of the oldest national organizations, AHS is a trusted source of gardening information and has a wonderful mission to provide education, social responsibility and environmental stewardship with the art and science of horticulture. Please consider joining to make "America a nation of gardeners and a land of gardens."

www.ahs.org/

County extension agents are a wealth of knowledge. I highly recommend attending seminars that your regional Master Gardeners put on as they are the best source for useful information for your specific climate and conditions. Join the Master Gardeners program to learn horticultural skills like a pro!

www.ahs.org/gardening-resources/master-gardeners

Volunteer at a school garden

Elementary and middle schools are an ideal location for foodscaping. The wide open campuses tend to have a lot of open space and full sun conditions. Children need to be exposed to how food is cultivated so they can grow into adults who value healthy eating habits and being good stewards of the Earth. From fund raising for the installation of foodscape campuses to volunteering at after school gardening programs – the possibilities are endless when working with public education. There are many organizations involved in installing school gardens.

growing-minds.org/school-gardens/
www.kidsgardening.org/
www.lifelab.org/for-educators/schoolgardens/

Public schools may be one of the best areas to develop foodscapes and positively impact your community. By combining the value of healthy eating and the science of horticulture we can inspire the next generation in a meaningful way. The Bullock Garden project in Glassboro, NJ, is a great example of how a horticulture initiative can positively influence society by creating a foodscaped teaching garden.

www.glassboroschools.us/Page/5168

Through a national collaboration known as Sustainable Heroes, headed up by celebrity landscaper and HGTV host Ahmed Hassan, we "school crashed" the property of Bullock Elementary. An unused courtyard was transformed into a bountiful classroom in one weekend. It was a career-changing experience for me in many ways. The excitement of the teachers, administrators and other volunteers filled me with the sense that horticultural knowledge is valuable and necessary. Hearing 500 children chant "Garden! Garden! Garden!" during a pep rally brought tears to my eyes and a sense of meaning I had never experienced before.

www.sustainableheroes.org/index.php

Thanks to the generosity of donors like Peace Tree Farms and Organic Mechanics Soil, this schoolyard garden is plentiful in its healthy production of fruits and vegetables. The school has partnered with the New Jersey Department of Agriculture's Jersey Fresh program to raise and serve Jersey Fresh produce in the cafeteria.

In 2016 teacher Sonya Harris was awarded the first ever New Jersey Department of Agriculture Farm to School award. The cafeteria at Glassboro's Dorothy L. Bullock School features produce grown in the school foodscape. Children have the opportunity to make salsa with ingredients grown in the garden and the school has an apple-tasting contest featuring local apples. The after-school garden club helps maintain the space throughout the school year. Twice a year, I have the pleasure of hosting garden-related pep rallies and teaching seed-sowing classes.

The NJ Agricultural Society trains teachers and provides free courses on how to incorporate garden lessons across the curriculum. Teachers use the garden as a space for instructing in writing and reading, in addition to teaching growing, harvesting and culinary skills. Under the supervision of teachers and Food Corps representatives, classes have a rotating schedule in the garden. The school plans to continue developing the garden classroom and STEM lab as an interactive, instructional learning hub.

Horticulture education belongs in every school system. Students will eat and learn from what they grow! Children relish time spent in a garden and edible classrooms are an excellent way to connect health, wellness and nutrition to horticulture. Horticulture professionals and home gardening enthusiasts alike have an incredible opportunity to team up with programs like Growing Minds to help train individuals to design and establish school foodscapes by integrating gardening into state and national curriculums.

It was during this experience that I realized designing and installing school gardens is the easy part. Schools need more help with long-term management, which is what I work on through my business, Brie Grows. Through this effort I work to connect professional horticulture resources to school gardening programs. From financial donations to growing advice, my goal is to support the staff and students to ensure a long lasting educational experience through horticultural ventures.

https://briegrows.com/

Each school is different and you can be of service in many different ways. Reach out to your local school district to understand their needs and to identify how your help and expertise can be best utilized.

Connect at home

If you live in a community with a homeowners association (HOA) communicate your desire to grow food with the members of the landscape committee by submitting a professional landscape plan that shows the permanent ornamental plants and the areas that will be used for growing fresh produce. Hire a designer to create a scaled drawing to show that you are installing a professional-quality landscape. If needed, hire the designer to be your advocate at the HOA meeting. Professional horticulturists can present the plan and maintenance strategy on your behalf and will have the capacity to answer all of the questions with a level of expertise. Remember that HOA covenants exist for a reason: to maintain high property values and ensure that the neighborhood looks tidy. The purpose of a foodscape is to meet those requirements while also providing you with fresh, nutritious food.

Get to know the people living nearest you and ask if they are interested in growing fresh produce. Gardening can be a lively, social hobby and seeing your neighbors out tending their crops is a great motivator.

Plan a neighborhood party where everyone brings a dish from their foodscape. We do this as a Fourth of July celebration; it is a fun way to share your harvests, recipes, advice and swap seeds!

Identify the green spaces in your neighborhood and see if it is possible for those areas to be managed as foodscapes. Neighborhood entries are a great place to start because everyone sees them. If they are professionally managed, ask your HOA advocates to communicate with the landscape contractor maintaining the site.

Hire professionals for success

The best way to increase awareness of The Foodscape Revolution is to involve horticulture professionals. The more people ask about growing food in conventional landscapes, the faster the green industry will react to meeting those needs. Hire professionals to help you plan, install and manage your foodscape to ensure the highest quality results.

Index

Abelia 116, 179

Abutilon 177

Acid/Acidic 33, 59, 87, 89, 111, 116, 120

Aeroponics 104

Aeroponics 141, 143

Agastache 34, 176

Almonds 92

Alyssum 26, 35

Amaranth 24, 50, 54, 55, 95

Amendments 23, 38, 40

Andromeda 180

Anise Hyssop 176

Apples 36, 88, 182

Aquaponics 141, 144

Aralia 179

Arborvitae 180

Aronia 26

Artichoke 50

Arugula 28, 47, 49, 50, 54, 55, 60, 119, 147, 153

Asparagus 50, 55, 62, 116, 160

Aster 176

Astilbe 176

Azalea 34, 116, 176, 177, 179

Barley 95, 124, 156

Barometerbush 179

Basil 26, 46, 49, 81, 119, 124, 147, 153, 157

Beautyberry 178

Bee Balm 178

Beet 26, 50, 55, 131

Big Bluestem 178

Biodiversity xvii, 31, 32, 94, 131, 172, 175

Bird of Paradise 179, 180

Blackberries 22, 89

Blackberry 24, 26

Bok Choy 6, 50, 56, 63

Bolt/Bolting 45, 60, 64, 70, 76, 80

Boxwood 116, 175, 178, 180

Bramble 89

Breath of Heaven 180

Broadcast sowing 53, 54

Broccoli 49, 50, 56, 63, 139, 147, 155, 157, 160

Brussels Sprouts 50

Buckwheat 26, 96, 156

Bugleweed 176

Burning Bush 180

Butcher's Broom 179

Butterfly Bush 178

Cabbage xi, xii, xvi, 33, 35, 41, 52, 63, 64, 66, 70, 108, 110, 131, 147, 155, 157

Cabbage worm xii

Calendula 35, 131

Calibrachoa 136, 137

Camellia 34, 116, 176, 177, 179, 180

Candytuft 179

Canning 159, 160, 165, 169, 170

Carex 136, 137, 138

Carrot 24, 26, 50, 54, 55, 65, 72, 124, 131, 160

Catmint 178

Cauliflower 49, 50, 56, 65, 147, 155, 157, 160

Cedar 175

Celery 50, 52, 56, 66, 153

Celosia 24, 26, 35

Cherry 24, 130, 143, 176, 177

Chestnut 24, 178

Chive 26, 28

Cilantro 26, 50, 54, 55, 82, 124, 153, 157

Clematis 178, 179

Cleome 26, 131

Clethra 176, 178

Coleus 26, 35

Collards 24, 50, 55, 56, 66, 160

Communal flats 57, 96, 100, 101

Compost 23, 25, 28, 29, 38, 40, 51, 65, 77, 80, 104, 120, 126, 130, 133

Cooperative Extension 37, 103, 108

Coral Bells 178

Coriander 82

Corn xiii, xiv, 24, 26, 45, 49, 50, 54, 55, 56, 66, 67, 124, 152, 153, 156, 157, 160

Cornflower 26

Cosmos 26

Cotoneaster 180

Crabapple 177, 178

Cranberry 177

Crape Myrtle 34, 176

Creeping Jenny 119

Cucumber 28, 47, 48, 50, 54, 67, 110, 118, 137, 147, 160

Cuphea 35

Currant 26, 177, 180

Cypress 176

Daylily 178

Dill 26, 82, 153

Direct sow 50, 52, 56, 65

Diseases 56, 63, 64, 76, 79, 107, 110, 139, 143, 146

Dogwood 180

Eastern Redbud 177

Echeveria 137

Edge/Edging 2, 33, 41, 46, 53, 55, 60, 69, 71, 72, 73, 75, 81, 116, 118, 119, 127, 135, 139, 171

Eggplant 26, 44, 49, 50, 55, 56, 68, 126, 131, 136, 147, 152, 158

Elephant Ear 175

Euphorbia 136

False Goat's Beard 178

False Lilac 179

Fennel 68

Fennel 50, 56, 68

Fertilizer 33, 37, 38, 73, 89, 100, 104, 105, 121, 133, 139, 140

Fig 121

Firebush 177

Index

Fire Pit 9, 115, 120, 121

Flax 180

Food miles xv, xvii, 44, 142

Foodscape zone 22, 39

Fothergilla 33, 175, 178

Foundation landscape ix, xvi, 21, 22, 27, 31, 33, 39, 46, 72, 73, 77, 95, 172

Fountain grass xvi

Fragrant Tea Olive 177

Garlic xv, 26, 28, 46, 50, 54, 55, 69, 71, 74, 76, 80, 119, 121, 158, 160, 166, 167, 168, 170

Geranium 176

Ginger 131, 177, 178

Gluten-free 92, 95

Gooseberry 26, 177

Grape 26, 176, 178

Guava, pineapple 176, 179

Hardening-off 57

Hazelnuts 92, 93

Hibiscus xvi, 179

HOA 1, xiii, xvi, 29, 123, 129, 171, 183

Holly/Hollies 6, 116, 130, 176, 179, 188

Homeowners Association xiii, 183

Honeyberry 24, 26

Honeysuckle 178, 180

Horseradish 24

Hosta 176

Hydrangea 33, 34, 48, 79, 106, 172, 175, 176, 177, 178, 179, 180

Hydroponic/Hydroponics 28, 116, 118, 141, 142, 144, 145

Hyssop 176

Indigo 179

Insects xv, 32, 70, 82, 84, 99, 109, 110

Iris 177

Jasmine 177

Kale ix, xvi, 26, 35, 44, 47, 49, 50, 55, 56, 57, 70, 118, 119, 121, 134, 147, 153, 160

Kangaroo Paws 180

Kiwi 177

Kohlrabi xii, 153

Kumquat 177, 180

Lantana 35

Larkspur 26, 53, 54, 101, 124, 126, 128, 131

Laurel 176, 180

Laurustinus 179

Lavender 83, 137

Leek 26

Lemon 177, 180

Lemongrass x, 180

Lettuce ix, xi, 2, 26, 27, 28, 33, 44, 45, 46, 47, 49, 50, 54, 55, 57, 60, 70, 71, 107, 115, 119, 121, 134, 137, 138, 145, 146, 147, 153

Lilac 176, 179

Lime 37, 38, 67, 81, 166, 176, 180

Loquat 180

Love-in-a-mist 54

Magnolia 179

Mandarin Orange 176, 177, 180

Marigold 35, 131

Meadow 9, 25, 45, 52, 53, 57, 94, 101, 123, 124, 125, 126, 127

Melampodium 35

Melon 91, 160

Milkweed 180

Million bells 137

Mistflower 179

Mizuna 50, 54, 55, 56, 71, 138

Mock Orange 179

Mountain Mint 179

Muhly Grass 177

Mulch ix, xiv, xvii, 23, 25, 27, 29, 38, 40, 41, 51, 53, 54, 65, 70, 99, 107, 120, 126, 127, 133, 139

Mustard Greens 24, 49, 50, 54, 55, 60, 131, 153

Natal Plum 177

Nectarine 180

Nematodes 62, 64, 76, 79, 107, 108, 110, 143

Nigella 124, 131

Ninebark 175

Nitrogen 37, 64, 72, 75, 104, 131

Oats xv, 26, 49, 50, 53, 54, 56, 57, 96, 97, 98, 126, 131, 156, 157

Okra xiv, xvi, 110

Onion xv, 26, 28, 46, 50, 55, 66, 71, 91, 119, 158, 160, 178

Orange 65, 153, 165, 176, 177, 178, 179, 180

Oregano 83, 119, 137, 153, 158, 167, 168

Organic xi, xiii, xiv, xv, 29, 33, 36, 37, 69, 71, 72, 77, 82, 88, 89, 96, 100, 104, 105, 107, 110, 120, 121, 126, 127, 130, 133, 139, 140, 144, 170, 171, 182, 187

Ornamental ix, x, xii, xiv, xv, xvi, 9, 22, 23, 25, 27, 31, 32, 33, 35, 36, 37, 43, 49, 52, 57, 63, 75, 84, 85, 92, 94, 97, 98, 100, 101, 116, 118, 120, 121, 123, 130, 131, 133, 136, 171, 175, 177, 178, 183, 188

Osmanthus 176, 177, 180

Pak Choi 50, 56, 63

Panama Rose 177

Pansies 63, 70, 138

Parsnip 24, 26, 55, 72, 131, 139

Passion Fruit 180

Paw Paw 24, 36, 90

Pea 50, 55, 74

Peach 24, 36, 88, 177

Peanuts xv, 32, 46, 72, 106, 119, 124, 128, 131, 155, 158, 161

Pear 36, 88, 176

Peas 74, 152

Pecan 24, 91, 93, 176

Penstemon 34

Peppers ix, xiv, xv, 26, 28, 44, 45, 46, 49, 50, 52, 56, 73, 75, 79, 106, 111, 119, 124, 126, 131, 136, 145, 147, 152, 158, 159, 160, 161, 169, 170, 172

Index

Perennials x, xiii, 22, 34, 43, 49, 119
Perilla xii, 35
Persimmon 22, 24, 90, 91, 116, 176, 178
Pest xi, xvii, 64, 75, 77, 107, 108, 111, 123
Petunia 33, 35, 136, 137
Phlox 119, 176, 178
Phosphorus 37, 64
Pine 89, 120, 123, 176
Plectranthus 136, 137
Plumbago 177
Pomegranate 176, 179
Poppies 53, 54, 101, 123, 126, 128, 131
Possumhaw 179
Potassium 37, 64, 72
Potato 26, 46, 47, 50, 55, 56, 68, 71, 75, 84, 119, 136, 137, 158
Pots 9, 27, 68, 70, 135, 136, 138, 139, 140
Princess Flower 177
Property screen 9, 25, 95, 123
Pruning 33
Pumpkin 47, 54, 134
Quince 33, 176, 179
Radish 76, 138
Raspberry 24, 26, 91
Rhubarb 24, 26, 44, 50, 177
Rice xvi, 28, 49, 50, 54, 55, 57, 64, 96, 97, 136, 156, 170
Rose 95, 116, 175, 177, 178, 179, 180
Rosemary 84, 137, 139, 153, 158, 179, 180
Rutabaga 24, 131
Rye 98, 124, 126
Sage 85, 139, 153, 158, 179
Salvia xiv, 35, 85, 179
Scallions 50, 55, 56
Sedge 136, 137, 138
Sedum 34, 137, 176
Serviceberry 130, 177, 178
Sesame 26, 64, 98, 99, 124, 126, 128, 156
Shallots 50, 55, 56, 74
Snapdragon 26, 35, 70, 131, 138
Sod 29, 41

Soilless growing 144
Soil test 37, 38, 51, 104, 108, 111
Sorghum xv, 24, 45, 49, 50, 55, 99, 124, 165, 170
Soybean 24, 26, 46, 49, 50, 54, 55, 75, 119, 124, 131
Spinach 28, 50, 55, 56, 71, 76, 91, 147, 153, 157, 160
Spiraea 116, 176, 179
Spruce 176, 180
Squash xiii, 28, 47, 48, 50, 54, 55, 77, 106, 110, 118, 119, 120, 131, 135, 140, 153, 160
Staking 74, 79, 106
St. John's Wort 179
Strawberry 47, 91, 119, 180
Succulents 137
Sumac 179
Summersweet 176, 178
Sunflower 24, 26, 50, 54, 55, 124, 131, 156
Sweet potato 75, 136, 155, 137
Sweet potato vine 136
Sweetspire 178, 179
Swiss Chard xvi, 26, 49, 50, 55, 56, 57, 118, 119, 121, 137, 138, 153, 157, 177
Thumbing-in 54
Thyme 85, 119, 137, 139, 153, 158, 167
Tickseed 176
Tomatillo 26, 49, 131
Tomato 28, 44, 48, 50, 56, 62, 78, 79, 83, 106, 108, 109, 110, 111, 131, 136, 137, 147, 158, 159, 160, 161, 164, 165, 166, 167, 168, 172
Torenia 137
Tower Garden 143
Transplants 23, 55, 56, 63, 66, 84, 133, 139
Trenches 55
Turnip 24, 26, 50, 55, 80, 131, 134, 139, 155
Twinberry 177
Viburnum 48, 177, 178, 179, 180
Vinca 136, 137
Viola 35, 131

Walnut 24
Watermelon 50, 54, 91, 131
Weigela 116, 175
Willow 179
Winterhazel 178
Wintersweet 179
Witch Hazel 178, 179
Yew 32, 34, 116, 175
Yucca 175
Zinnia 24, 26, 35, 124, 126, 131
Zucchini 77, 104, 119, 131, 146, 153, 160

Recipes:
Brie's Homegrown Bloody Mary 166
Candied Jalapeño Peppers 169
Heirloom Tomato Juice 165
Pizza Sauce 167
Practical Heirloom Tomato Paste 166
Spaghetti Sauce 168

Acknowledgments

The Foodscape Revolution has been a decade in the making. As a professional grower and propagator with a passion for cultivating organic produce, it is an honor and a privilege to share my experience and knowledge. The act of growing food holds so much meaning to every person on the Earth; from understanding how to germinate a seed to learning to harvest and prepare the crops you have cultivated, foodscaping represents the value of life in every single landscape.

My foodscape passion could not have taken shape without the loving support and unwavering encouragement from my husband, David Arthur. When we broke ground at our current home on January 3, 2011, I recall declaring "The work has just begun!" Little did we know that from those first plantings a philosophy of land use would grow to reinvent the purpose of everyday landscapes. David, I love you and am grateful to have you in my life as a partner, chef and innovator.

Some of my first memories are of summer days in my grandparents' suburban Pittsburgh garden where they grew more food than I could imagine, along with world-class Rhododendrons and perfectly hedged boxwoods – all edged with the most magnificent lawn in their neighborhood. Growing plants was second nature to them and it had a profound impact on me.

While growing up in southeastern Michigan, my wonderful parents, Dan and Lynn Gluvna, had the good sense to enroll me in 4-H. I will never forget

earning a county fair blue ribbon in the cut flower competition for my entry of *Echinops ritro*, the first botanical name I learned to spell and pronounce! Looking back, it was those long, hot days at the Monroe County Fair that solidified my love for and interest in horticulture. Thank you, Mom and Dad, for your love and support, and for taking me to 4-H meetings all those years!

My passion for growing plants was truly realized in the summer of 1999, when, as an intern, I had the good fortune to work for Jeff Mast, then manager of Heartland Growers. His encouragement and kindness gave me the confidence to follow my dreams and pursue a career as a professional grower and propagator. Despite the many challenges along the way, that experience as a 19-year-old intern will always provide motivation to push the boundaries and promote the value that plants offer.

The Foodscape Revolution is a movement for the next generation. Children deserve the opportunity to experience the outdoors and explore their natural curiosity about how and where food is grown. My dearest garden helpers,

Aidan and Abby DelGatto, exemplify this notion and I am so thankful they came into my life and participate in the daily foodscape management throughout our neighborhood. Watching them learn important life lessons such as healthy eating habits and the value of exercise has inspired me to reach out to public school systems across the U.S.

Working with talented educators like Sonya Harris has made the transition into public school systems possible. Garden education belongs in EVERY school, and by engaging students in hands-on learning in the foodscape, lessons can be taught across the curriculum. To everyone at the award-winning Bullock Elementary School: THANK YOU for all that you do to educate the next generation!

Raising the bar for the average landscape is a big task. Thank you, Erin Weston, owner of Weston Farms, for your support, encouragement and friendship and for proving that untraditional businesses can succeed. Without the support of colleagues within the Green Industry my voice and message would never be heard. I am so grateful to everyone involved in American Hort, FNGLA, GWA, IPPS, NCNLA and OAN for providing the opportunities for me to preach the Foodscaping message and connect with other professionals who are actively making this a national movement.

A very special thank-you to Growing A Greener World TV and Joe Lamp'l, who arrived in my foodscape on a hot July day in 2014 and changed my life. Participating in a nationally syndicated PBS television series is truly a career high.

Sincerest thanks to all of the contributors of The Foodscape Revolution, including plant professionals from around the U.S., whose regional plant lists help guide the selection of ornamental specimens for the foodscape. I am so grateful to consider each of you friends and colleagues: Angela Treadwell-Palmer, Janet Draper, Barbara Katz, Preston Montague, Jenks Farmer, Bobby Green, Teresa Watkins, Maria Zampini, Christa Steenwyk, Kelly D. Norris, Caleb Melchior, Jared Barnes, Leslie Finical Halleck, Todd Lasseigne, Panayoti Kelaidis, Rizanino Reyes and Wendy Shinar. Chef Emily Peterson, thank you for inspiring me with your culinary expertise.

Much appreciation to Paul Kelly and Cathy Dees of St. Lynn's Press for taking this project on and being patient and kind through my writing process. Thank you, Holly Rosborough, for your artistic direction – and to the brilliant designer and illustrator Preston Montague for providing colorful, realistic drawings of my home foodscape to inspire readers to create a living landscape that is beautiful and bountiful.

Finally, my eternal gratitude to Katie Elzer-Peters for making this book come to life. Without you, The Foodscape Revolution would still be a PowerPoint presentation. Thank you for your patience and capacity to read my mind and articulate the foodscaping message in a thoughtful and easy-to-apply manner. You are a talented writer, horticulturist, generous friend, and you truly make this world a better place.

About the Author

Originally from southeastern Michigan, Brie Arthur studied Landscape Design and Horticulture at Purdue University. She has more than a decade of experience in plant production at leading nurseries. Today, she conveys her love of plants and design through her writing, speaking, film production and consulting. Brie is an inspired, creative advocate for the value of horticulture in our lives – both for the green industry and the public.

As a professional communicator, Brie is leading the national suburban Foodscape movement, a model of community development that incorporates sustainable, local food production. Working with commercial and residential design, and with public school systems and municipalities, Brie is changing the way green spaces are planned and utilized. She is a correspondent on the PBS television show Growing A Greener World, sharing practical advice from her one-acre suburban foodscape, and encouraging everyone to embrace the hobby and lifestyle of home gardening.

Brie serves as the GWA (Garden Writers Association) National Director of Region IV, representing garden communicators across the southeast U.S. A founding member of Emergent: A Group For Growing Professionals, she encourages an open dialogue and networking opportunities between seasoned professionals and rising green industry members. Brie sits on the Executive Committee for the International Plant Propagators Society Southern Region and is on the board of directors for the North Carolina Botanical Garden Foundation.

https://briegrows.com

OTHER BOOKS FROM ST. LYNN'S PRESS

www.stlynnspress.com

Good Bug Bad Bug
by Jessica Walliser
104 pages • Hardback
ISBN: 978-0981961590

Garden-Pedia
by Pamela Bennett and Maria Zampini
224 pages • Paperback
ISBN: 978-0989268844

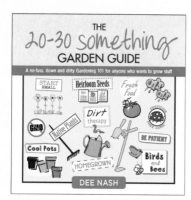

The 20-30 Something Garden Guide
by Dee Nash
160 pages, Hardback
ISBN: 978-0985562274

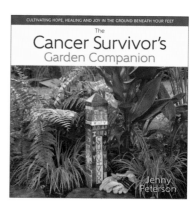

The Cancer Survivor's Garden Companion
by Jenny Peterson
192 pages • Hardback
ISBN: 978-0989268899